THE ORI
Vidalia Onion
COOKBOOK

Recipes Compiled and Tested
by Pam McIntyre, Food Editor
(Unless otherwise indicated)

TOOMBS COUNTY

Chamber of Commerce

Printed in the USA by
WIMMER
The Wimmer Companies, Inc.
Memphis

© 1981, TOOMBS COUNTY CHAMBER OF COMMERCE   ISBN 0-9651862-0-2

VIDALIA SWEET ONIONS

This unusually mild and succulent onion is the Yellow Granex Type F Hybrid, which is also grown in many other parts of the country. However, when combined with our South Georgia climate and the soil in the Vidalia area, the Granex matures into what has become a gourmet's favorite—The Vidalia Sweet Onion.

The delicate nature of the Vidalia Onion requires it be harvested by hand and treated gently when it is graded and packed. The supply of Vidalia Onions is quite limited because they can only be grown in a small area surrounding Vidalia, Georgia, and because of the large amount of labor required for harvest. Since demand for our onions has become so widespread, it is sometimes difficult to fill all requests.

Since Vidalia Onions are available only during a short time each year, many people buy in quantity (50 to 100 pounds) and store them for extended enjoyment. Storing Vidalia Onions is a challenge, and it must be done with care. To store them successfully, the two main requirements are a cool, dry area and air circulation. The two most popular methods are: (1) Storing them in the legs of old panty hose by tying a knot between each onion and (2) storing them on racks made of window screen or air conditioner filters making sure the onions do not touch one another. They have been stored successfully for extended periods, but the onion's relative sugar and moisture content make this a difficult undertaking.

The Vidalia Onions were first produced commercially in the Vidalia area in the early 1940's and promoted through the Vidalia State Farmer's Market. At that time, the Vidalia State Farmer's Market was the central point for onion growers and buyers. As reorders were made, they were referred to as "Vidalia Onions."

Harvest usually begins around the first of May and usually continues until about mid-June. Onions are usually shipped in 10, 25, or 50 pound bags and are available in small, medium, and jumbo sizes.

Additional information about the onion's availability can be obtained by contacting the Vidalia Chamber of Commerce, Vidalia, Georgia.

Foreword

The Onion season is a festive time for all Vidalians. The seeds are planted, the onions are made, and done up in onion growers bags, while joy and laughter abound amist the hustle and bustle of our onion season. It is, above all, a time when young and old alike delight in sharing the activities that give Vidalians their own unique and special spirit.

Homey simplicity is the heart of this festive occasion, from down-to-earth naturalness of French fried onion rings, Vidalia Onion Cookoff, Vidalia Onion Cooking School, and Arts and Crafts Festival, to the old fashioned charm of square dancing, having a Vidalia Onion Beauty Queen, etc.—and the whole Vidalia Onion Festival. It all adds up to an easy and fun festival that everyone in the family enjoys.

For most Vidalians the holidays mean getting together with family and friends to share special food and customs. All across Toombs County families celebrate the season with their own style of food and fellowship.

On the following pages we show meals you can serve your family to make your holiday gatherings special. Plus we've included a section of recipes for appetizers; soups, salads, salad dressings, bread/pastas/rice, entrees, and vegetables/pastas casseroles so you can put together your own menus or fill out a menu you have already planned.

We Vidalians are profoundly lucky. Not only do we have a Vidalia Onion tradition native to our own soil, but also we've fallen heir to a vast treasure of arts and crafts festival brought to our shores from other countries by many waves of new citizens. Why not celebrate the Vidalia Onion Season by cooking, using our onion cookbook.

Pam Mc Intyre
Food Editor

Miss Pam McIntyre is a Bachelor of Science graduate of the University of Georgia. Currently she is employed by Meadows Memorial Hospital, Vidalia, Georgia where she is Director of Dietetics. She also is a Renal Consultant for the Candler County Renal Dialysis Center, Metter, Georgia and The Southern States Nephrology Center, Eastman, Georgia.

DEDICATION

Philippians 4:8

Finally, Brethren, whatever is true, whatever is honorable, whatever is just, whatever is pure, whatever is lovely, whatever is gracious, if there is any excellence, if there is anything worthy of praise, think about these things.

I dedicate this book to the People of Vidalia with love and appreciation for the interest and encouragement they have given to me.

Pam McIntyre

Table of Contents

APPETIZERS

Appetizers are those pleasantly tantalizing light finger foods served with drinks before a meal. Serve a variety of simple appetizers to provide appropriate color, texture, and flavor. Hors d'oeuvres set your mood whether it be elegance and richness or on a lesser, but nontheless, appetizing plane.

A smart hostess can make appetizers in advance with planned shopping and preparation. Hot hors d'oeuvres may be prepared ahead and reheated in the chafing dish at serving time.

Cheese straws, pastries, fresh vegetables, and various fruits can be prepared ahead of time and stored in proper containers in a cool place. Crisp certain food for two minutes in hot oven before serving. Fill according to recipe and serve right away.

●

SOUPS

There are hot and cold soups to fit a variety of menus and serving styles—from very casual to elegant.

SOUTH CAROLINA PICKLED ONIONS

Peel small white onions, cover with brine, using 1½ cups salt, with 2 quarts boiling water. Let get cold. Let stand 2 days. Drain, make vinegar, using 1 cup sugar to half gallon, pour over hot onions, boiling hot, fill to overflowing, seal while hot. Vidalia Onions pickled in this way are considered a real delicacy.

———————•———————

CREAM OF ONION AND CELERY SOUP

1½ cups minced Vidalia Onions
½ cup minced celery
1 cup hot chicken bouillon
½ tsp. salt
3 tbsps. butter
3 tbsps. flour
2 cups hot milk
1 tsp. salt
¼ tsp. freshly ground pepper
⅛ tsp. ground nutmeg
½ cup heavy cream, heated
1-2 tbsps. chopped pistachio nuts

Combine the onion, celery, hot chicken bouillon, and salt. Simmer, covered, until the onion and celery are very soft. Rub through a sieve, put through a food mill, or puree' in the blender. Heat the butter in a saucepan and stir in the flour. Gradually blend in until smooth and thickened. Add the salt, pepper, nutmeg and pureed vegetables. Cook until heated through. Stir in the hot cream. Sprinkle with chopped pistachio nuts. Serves 4.

ANGUS FANCY ONIONS

Brought home from Scotland by Vidalians who find the recipe even better when made with Vidalia Sweet Onions.

4 large Vidalia Onions, sliced
⅛ lb. butter (½ stick)
1½ cups bread crumbs
½ tsp. salt
¼ tsp. pepper
1 tsp. dry English mustard
1½ cups grated cheese (American or Swiss)

Fry onions in the butter until light brown. Transfer to a casserole dish. Combine the bread crumbs, salt, pepper and mustard. Spread over the onions in the casserole dish. Sprinkle the cheese over mixture. Bake until cheese is melted, about 20 minutes at 350⁰. Serves 4.

———————•———————

PIMENTO-ONION RELISH

⅓ cup vinegar
½ tsp. fine herbs
2 tbsps. sugar
⅔ cup water
1-4 oz. can or jar whole pimentos, quartered
1 medium Vidalia Onion, thinly sliced (about 1 cup)

Combine vinegar, fine herbs, sugar and water. Add pimentos and onion; marinate overnight. Drain; serve with meat.

SPICY PICKLED ONION RINGS

4 cups onion rings (about 1 pound), sliced and separated into rings, 1-16 oz. can beets, 1½ cups white vinegar, ¼ cup sugar, ½ tsp. salt, 6 inches stick cinnamon (broken up), 2 tsps. whole cloves. Drain beets, reserving juice; add enough water to make 1½ cups. Add the vinegar, sugar, salt, cinnamon, and cloves. Simmer covered for 10 minutes. Strain; pour hot mixture over onions, chill several hours or overnight. Drain before serving.

——————— • ———————

GOOD ONION RELISH

3 large Vidalia Onions
12 Red Peppers (Bell)
12 Green Peppers (Bell)
1 Hot Pepper

Chop all very fine; put into boiling water and boil 20 minutes. Drain. Pour boiling water over contents of pot and boil again 15 minutes; drain, and add:
1 tbsp. salt
1 cup brown sugar
1 quart white vinegar
Boil 10 minutes and put in jars and seal while hot.

——————— • ———————

ONION RELISH

Grind onions to make 3 gallons, sprinkle with 1 cup salt, and let stand 30 to 40 minutes; squeeze out most of the juice. To ½ gallon vinegar, add spices to taste. (About 2 tsps. tumeric, pickling spices, pimento, and 4 lbs. sugar). Pour over onions and cook 30 minutes stirring constantly. Put in hot jars and seal.

FRENCH ONION SOUP

4 medium Vidalia Onions, chopped
1 cup butter
1¼ cup flour, all-purpose
6 cups homemade beef stock
1 tsp. salt
½ tsp. white pepper
3 tbsps. cream
1 egg yolk
buttered croutons
parmesan cheese

Melt 2 tbsps. butter in a large soup pot. Add onions and lower heat. Cook onions until tender. Add butter and flour, cook until golden. Add stock, salt and pepper. Beat cream and egg yolk together. Add a little hot soup to mixture, blend, then pour back into soup. If too thick, add more water. To serve pour in bowls, add croutons and sprinkle with cheese.

ONION VEGETABLE SOUP WITH GROUND BEEF

1 lb. lean ground beef
2 cups Vidalia Onions, chopped
1 can kidney beans
1 cup sliced carrots
1 cup green pepper, chopped
¼ cup uncooked rice
1 cup chopped celery
1 can stewed tomatoes
2 cups water
3 beef bouillon cubes
1 tbsp. chopped parsley
½ tsp. salt
¼ tsp. basil
dash of red pepper
Cook beef and onion until brown. Drain off fat. Combine other ingredients and simmer in fryer or crock pot. Cover and cook for 2 or 3 hours. Serve hot.

TOMATO/ONION SOUP

6 medium Vidalia Onions, peeled and sliced
1½ lbs. butter
2 tbsps. flour
1 qt. beef consomme'
1 cup white wine
12 large ripe tomatoes, chopped and peeled
¼ tsp. rosemary
¼ tsp. thyme
Parsley and sour cream as a garnish

Saute' onions in butter; add flour, consomme', wine, tomatoes and seasonings and simmer for 1 hour. Process in food processor until smooth. Strain through cheesecloth. Return to pan and reheat. Garnish with parsley and sour cream. Serve immediately.

———— • ————

ONION AND MUSHROOM SOUP

4 tbsps. butter
1 medium Vidalia Onion, chopped
2 cups fresh mushrooms or 8 oz. can mushrooms, drained
1-11 oz. can cream of mushroom soup
1 tbsp. catsup
1-11 oz. can beef consomme'
1-6 oz. can tomato juice
¾ cup heavy cream
2-3 tbsps. parsley

Saute' onions and mushrooms in butter. Add other ingredients (setting aside cream and parsley) and bring to a boil for 3 or 4 minutes. Lower heat and simmer. Before serving, add cream and parsley. 6 to 8 servings.

GROUND BEEF ONION DIP

1 lb. ground beef
2 medium Vidalia Onions, chopped
1 cup sliced mushrooms
1 cup sliced water chestnuts
1 small can cream of chicken soup
3 cups cheese, mild American, grated

Brown ground beef, add onions, mushrooms, water chestnuts, cream of chicken soup and cheese. Simmer for 1 hour and serve with chips or fritos.

———— • ————

ONION PEPPER RELISH

Grind 8 hot peppers, 12 bell peppers, 10 large sweet onions; drain and squeeze out most of the juice. Add 5 cups vinegar, 5½ cups sugar and 3 tbsps. salt. Bring to a good boil and continue cooking until thick. Pour into jars and seal.

———— • ————

CRABMEAT AND ONION SOUP

1 tbsp. butter
1 medium Vidalia Onion, chopped
1 can cream of chicken soup
1 can beef consomme'
1 can white crabmeat
1 small can mushrooms, drained
1 can sliced water chestnuts, drained
⅓ cup sherry
⅔ cup water
Salt and pepper to taste

Saute' onions in butter. Put onions in remaining ingredients in sauce and cook over medium heat for 5 to 10 minutes. Serve hot. May be prepared the day before serving.

SMOOTH ONION SOUP
Rich and Delicious!

7 tbsps. butter
7 tbsps. flour
½ cup milk
½ cup light cream
2½ cups chicken broth
1 cup finely chopped onions
dash of white pepper

Melt butter in saucepan and saute' onions. Blend in flour, stirring. Remove from heat and add liquid ingredients. Return to heat and cook, stirring constantly until mixture thickens and comes to a boil; reduce heat. Return to boiling and serve immediately.

ONION BISQUE

3 cups onions, diced
2 cups milk
½ tsp. dill weed
½ tsp. Beau Monde Seasoning
4 tbsps. butter
3 tsps. cornstarch
1 tbsp. cold water

Clean onions and mix milk, dill weed and onions in 2 tbsps. butter in a saucepan. Heat until boiling on medium heat. Add butter and Beau Monde Seasoning. Mix cornstarch and water, stir into hot Bisque, keep warm. Sprinkle with dill weed for garnish.

ONION/VEGETABLE CHOWDER

4 large Vidalia Onions, chopped
4 large potatoes, diced
2 sticks butter
2 cups carrots, diced
1 cup green pepper, diced
1 cup celery, diced
3 cups Half & Half
3 tbsps. flour
2 cups hot chicken stock
Salt and pepper to taste

Saute' onions, potatoes, carrots, green pepper, and celery in 4 tbsps. butter and 3 tbsps. flour, chicken stock, Half & Half, salt, and pepper to taste. Simmer for 30 minutes on low heat. Add more Half & Half or milk if too thick.

CREAM OF ONION SOUP

¼ cup Vidalia Green Onions, tops
4 cups Vidalia Onions, thinly sliced
½ cup celery, diced
2 tbsps. butter
¼ tsp. salt
3 tbsps. uncooked rice
2 cups chicken broth
½ cup cream
Dash coarse black pepper

Place 2¼ cups onions, celery, salt, pepper and butter in a 2-quart saucepan; simmer for about 3 minutes on medium heat. Add broth and simmer for 15 minutes. DO NOT BOIL. Pour all in blender and liquify. Return to saucepan. Add remaining onions and cream.

PAM'S CRAB WITH ONIONS

2-6 oz. pkgs. frozen crabmeat, thawed and
   drained or canned
3 hard boiled eggs, chopped
3 medium Vidalia Onions, chopped, green
   onions
1 tsp. Worcestershire Sauce
¼ cup sour cream
¼ tsp. paprika
½ cup mayonnaise
Juice of ½ lemon

Break up crabmeat and add seasonings.
Toss lightly with sour cream. May serve
with crackers or stuffed in tomatoes for
a delightful appetizer.

ONION DIP

1 cup sour cream
½ cup Vidalia Onions, chopped
¼ tsp. parsley
¼ tsp. chives
⅛ tsp. thyme
¼ tsp. mustard, prepared

Mix together and serve with chips or
crackers.

BAKED ONIONS

4 medium onions
1 tbsp. Worcestershire Sauce
1 tbsp. butter
¼ tbsp. salt
Dash of pepper
Dash of garlic salt, if desired
1 tsp. cream cheese

Wash and clean onions, slit 4 times in
top ⅛ to ¼ inch. Add other ingredients
and cook until tender in 350⁰ F. oven
20 to 30 minutes. The ingredients in the
above mentioned recipe are to be added
individually to each of the 4 medium
onions.

SHRIMP ONION SPREAD OR DIP

1-8 oz. pkg. of cream cheese
2 cups finely diced shrimp, cooked and
   deveined
¼ tsp. paprika
½ tsp. prepared mustard
1 tsp. Worcestershire Sauce
1 small onion, grated
¼ cup mayonnaise

Beat cream cheese until smooth. Add
other ingredients. Can be served hot or
cold with crackers. If served hot, cook
at 350⁰ F. for 20 minutes and top with
2 tbsps. butter and 1 cup bread crumbs.
Use in a chafing dish and serve with
crackers, fritos, or chips.

————— • —————

ONION HAM CHOWDER

2 cups onions, chopped
2 tbsps. butter
1½ cups chicken broth
1 cup cream
1 can cream of potato soup
¼ cup water
2 tbsps. cornstarch
¼ tsp. coarsely ground black pepper
3 cups ham, cooked and diced
Parsley to garnish

Cook onions in butter until tender and
drain. In a bowl, mix cream and cream
of potato soup. Blend water, cornstarch,
and pepper; cook stirring occasionally
until thick and bubbly. Stir in ham;
simmer 15 minutes. Garnish with
parsley.

ONION-CHEESE BALL

1 medium Vidalia Onion, chopped
½ cup bacon, fried and crumbled
1 cup mild American cheese, grated
½ cup Monterey Jack cheese, grated
½ cup mild Swiss cheese, grated
½ cup Caraway Seed cheese, grated
8 oz. pkg. cream cheese
1 cup almonds or pecans, optional

Beat cream cheese until smooth and add other ingredients. Roll in pecans or almonds if desired.

————— • —————

OYSTER STEW WITH ONIONS

1 gallon milk
1 qt. oysters
1 tbsp. salt
½ tsp. pepper, white
½ to ¾ cup butter
1 cup diced Vidalia Onions

Scald milk and add oysters, onions, butter and pepper. Cook until edge of oysters begin to curl. Add salt just before serving. Makes 15 servings.

————— • —————

ONION HAM CHEESE SPREAD

½ cup chopped pecans
¾ cup ham, sandwiched, shredded or
  chopped fine
2 cups grated mild American cheese
¼ cup pecans (optional)
1 medium Vidalia Onion, chopped
8 oz. cream cheese

Beat cream cheese and add other ingredients. Roll cheese ball in pecans that have been set aside.

ONION SOUP

2 cups peeled and diced Vidalia Onions
1 qt. beef broth
1 cup heavy cream
Shredded cheese and croutons if desired
½ tsp. salt
¼ tsp. freshly ground pepper
2 egg yolks, beaten
1 tbsp. butter

Cook the onions in the beef broth until tender. Drain reserving liquid. Puree' and sieve the onions. Add the reserved broth to the pure'ed onions and bring to a boil. Remove from heat, add cream, season with salt and pepper. Reheat, do not boil. Remove from heat and stir in egg yolks and butter. Serve piping hot. Can garnish with shredded cheese and croutons.

ONION DILL SOUP

3 large Vidalia Onions, sliced
1 medium tomato, diced
1 small clove garlic
1 tsp. salt
¼ tsp. freshly ground black pepper
2 sprigs fresh dill
2 tbsps. tomato paste
¼ cup cold water
½ cup cooked macaroni
1 cup chicken stock
¾ cup Half & Half

Peel diced tomato in a saucepan. Add the onions, garlic, salt, pepper, dill, tomato paste and water. Cook and simmer 12 to 15 minutes. Transfer to electric blender. Add macaroni, cover and turn to high. Add stock and Half & Half, slowly and mix. Chill and serve. Garnish with fresh dill and chopped tomato.

NEW ENGLAND CLAM CHOWDER

4½ dozen medium hard-shelled clams
6½ cups cold water
1 2-inch cube salt pork, diced
2 medium Vidalia Onions, chopped
5 medium potatoes, diced
½ tsp. salt
¼ tsp. pepper, black freshly ground
2 cups milk
1 cup Half & Half

Wash clams thoroughly. Place them in a deep saucepan with the cold water. Bring to a boil and let boil gently for 10 minutes, or until the shells pop open. The water should almost cover the clams. Strain the broth through cheesecloth and reserve. Remove clams from shells, clean and chop. Fry the salt pork in the deep saucepan. Add the onion and cook slowly until it begins to turn golden brown. Add the clams and reserved broth. Skim well, if necessary. Add the potatoes and season with salt and pepper. Cook potatoes until tender. Remove from heat and slowly add the milk and Half & Half, which have been heated. Serve immediately.

———— • ————

CREAM OF ONION SOUP

1 10½-oz. can cream of chicken soup
1 medium Vidalia Onion, chopped
1 cup Cheddar cheese, grated
1 cup croutons

Mix first two ingredients together and heat until hot and bubbly. Add cheese and heat until it melts. Top with croutons. Serve immediately.

QUICK ONION SOUP

1 can onion soup
1 large Vidalia Onion, chopped
1 cup croutons
2 cups Cheddar cheese, grated

Boil onion soup and onions. Pour in cups and add cheese and croutons. Serve immediately.

———— • ————

STUFFED CELERY

4 ribs celery, washed, cleaned and
  cut in 4-inch sticks (length)
1 8-oz. pkg. cream cheese
1 tbsp. chives
¼ tsp. lemon juice
2 tbsps. chopped onions

Clean celery. Beat cream cheese and other ingredients together. Stuff celery. Garnish with sprigs of parsley and paprika if desired.

———— • ————

CHEESE ONION CHIPS

1 4-oz. pkg. potato chips
¾ cup grated Cheddar cheese
1 tbsp. poppy seed
½ tsp. thyme
½ cup chopped onion

Start oven at moderate heat (350° F.). Spread potato chips on baking sheets greased with PAM. Sprinkle with cheese and onions, then poppy seeds and thyme. Heat 5 to 8 minutes or until cheese is melted. Serve hot. Can use blue cheese or Swiss cheese to vary the flavor.

CHEESE ONION PUFFS

16 crisp Ritz crackers
1 small Vidalia Onion, chopped
1 egg, separated
1 tbsp. mayonnaise
⅛ tsp. salt
¼ tsp. pepper
16 pecan halves
Whiz cheese spread

Start oven at moderate heat (350° F.) Mix onions with cheese spread until creamy. Spread crackers with cheese mixture and arrange on a cookie sheet. Beat egg yolk until lemony. Mix with mayonnaise, salt and pepper. Whip egg white until stiff. Fold into yolk mixture. Heap on crackers. Bake 13 to 15 minutes or until top is set and browned. Serve hot. Makes about 16 puffs. Garnish with a pecan.

BACON ONION CANAPÉS

1 8-oz. pkg. cream cheese
1 large Vidalia Onion, chopped
2 tbsps. mayonnaise
¼ tsp. thyme
1 tbsp. chives
18 2-inch rounds cut from thin bread slices
4 slices lean bacon
Softened butter

Blend cream cheese, onion, mayonnaise, thyme, and chives. Use cookie cutter to cut rounds from thin slices of bread. Spread rounds with softened butter, then with cream cheese mixture. Cut bacon crosswise into 6 pieces each. Lay a piece of bacon on top and chill until serving time. Broil canapes 2 inches from broiler, heat until bacon is crisp, browned or curled. Serve at once.

CHEESE ONION BALL

½ cup Swiss cheese, grated
½ cup Monterey Jack cheese, grated
½ cup mild American cheese, grated
8-oz. pkg. cream cheese
¼ cup toasted sesame seeds
½ tsp. Worcestershire Sauce
½ cup Vidalia Onions, chopped
1 cup nuts, chopped

Beat cream cheese until smooth. Add cheeses and all other ingredients, except nuts. Shape into ball and roll in nuts. Serve with crackers.

ONION CANAPÉS

1 8-oz. pkg. cream cheese
2 cups Parmesan cheese
1 medium Vidalia Onion, peeled
  and chopped
Crisp crackers
Pecan halves

Mix cream cheese and Parmesan cheese to consistency of softened butter. Place a little chopped onion in center of crackers and top with mixture and place a pecan half on top. Place under broiler until puffed and brown. Serve immediately.

ONION SPREAD

1 8-oz. pkg. cream cheese
4 strips crumbled bacon
½ cup Vidalia Onions, chopped
1 tbsp. chives
2 tbsps. sour cream

Beat cream cheese until fluffy. Add other ingredients and serve with chips or crackers.

STUFFED TOMATOES

6 large tomatoes
2 lbs. bacon
½ cup finely chopped Vidalia Onions
½ cup mayonnaise
½ cup cheese, grated

Dice bacon and fry until crisp. Drain and cool. In a medium bowl, mix bacon, onions and mayonnaise. Remove tomato stems and cut slightly with kitchen shears and stuff with mixture. Top with cheese and melt in oven.

CHEESE LOG

2 cups Cheddar cheese, shredded
4-oz. cream cheese, room temp.
1 tbsp. parsley, chopped
1 medium Vidalia Onion, chopped
¼ cup pimento, finely chopped
¼ tsp. salt
¼ tsp. garlic salt
1 tsp. soy sauce
½ tsp. Tabasco Sauce
½ cup finely chopped pecans

Beat cream cheese until smooth, add other ingredients slowly, until all is added except nuts. Roll into a ball and roll in nuts. If nuts stick to hands, grease with mayonnaise or butter.

DIP

1 8-oz. pkg. cream cheese
1 5-oz. pkg. blue cheese, crumbled
2 tbsps. onion, grated
1 tbsp. capers, cut finely
1 tsp. Worcestershire Sauce
½ cup chopped pecans

Beat cream cheese until smooth, add other ingredients and chill. Serve with crackers.

SHRIMP SOUP

1 medium Vidalia Onion, chopped
1 large carrot, diced
¼ tsp. thyme
1 bay leaf
1 tbsp. green pepper, chopped
1 tbsp. chopped parsley
3 tbsps. chopped celery
3 tbsps. butter
1½ lbs. shrimp
4½ cups chicken broth
¼ cup dry white wine
½ cup raw rice

Saute' onion, carrots, thyme, bay leaf, pepper, parsley and celery in butter until slightly browned. Shell and devein shrimp. Cook covered in 1 cup of broth and wine for 5 minutes. Remove bay leaf. Strain, sieve and puree in blender. Add ground shrimp to the strained soup or keep whole if desired. Reheat and season with salt and pepper. Add the remaining butter and the shrimp as garnish.

———— • ————

SHRIMP AND ONIONS

2 lbs. boiled shrimp, hulled
3 medium Vidalia Onions, thinly sliced
¾ cup vinegar
1 cup catsup
¼ cup olive oil
¼ cup Parmesan cheese
¼ tsp. lemon juice
1 tsp. basil
1 tsp. coarsely ground black pepper

Mix together and chill. Serve cold with crackers.

BEEF ONION SPREAD

1 pkg. dried beef, finely chopped
1 8-oz. pkg. softened cream cheese
1 medium Vidalia Onion, chopped
½ cup chopped pecans
¼ tsp. cayenne pepper
1 tbsp. sour cream

Beat cream cheese until smooth, add other ingredients. Serve with crackers. Can serve hot at 325⁰ F. in oven for 20 minutes or serve cold.

CHEESE ONION SPREAD

1 cup crumbled blue cheese
1 cup graded cheddar cheese
1 cup sour cream
1 tbsp. onion, grated
1 tbsp. soy sauce
1 tsp. paprika
½ tsp. chives
½ tsp. parsley flakes
1 cup chopped almonds

Mash cheese. Blend with sour cream and seasonings with a fork or in a blender until smooth. Add almonds. Makes about 2¼ cups. Serve on crisp crackers.

HOT CRAB WITH ONIONS

1 16-oz. can crab, drained & checked
 for shells
1 small Vidalia Onion, chopped
1 can cream of chicken soup
2 cups grated mild American cheese
¼ tsp. paprika
½ cup mushrooms, sliced and drained
1 cup water chestnuts, sliced
1 can French Fried Onion Rings

Mix all ingredients except onion rings together and bake at 350⁰ F. for 30 to 40 minutes. Top with French Fried Onion Rings if desired. Brown, serve hot.

ONIONS WITH A CHEESE SAUCE

4 medium Vidalia Onions, sliced
3 tbsps. butter
SAUCE:
1 tbsp. flour
1 to 2 cups milk
1 cup cheese, grated
Garnish - fresh parsley, paprika

Saute' onions in butter until translucent. Sauce: Melt butter and add flour, milk, and cook over low heat. If too thick, add water and then add cheese. Pour over saute'ed onions and serve immediately. Garnish with fresh parsley or paprika.

———— • ————

GUACAMOLE

1 cup mashed avocado
1 tbsp. fresh lime juice
½ tsp. salt
1 tbsp. grated onion
½ tsp. Worcestershire Sauce
¼ cup crumbled Roquefort cheese
½ cup pimento, chopped

Blend all ingredients together smoothly with hand mixer. Use with Doritos or Fritos.

———— • ————

HAM DIP

3 tbsps. cream cheese
1 tbsp. sour cream
2 tsps. horseradish
2 cups chopped, cooked ham

Mix ingredients together. Spoon on pancake. Roll and fasten with toothpick. Heat under moderate broiler for 2 minutes or saute' lightly in butter in a chafing dish. Serve hot.

HAMBURGER ONION STRUDEL

1 lb. hamburger meat
1 lb. mushrooms, fresh & sliced
1 8 oz. pkg. softened cream cheese
½ cup chopped pecans
¼ tsp. cayenne pepper
1 tbsp. sour cream
1 medium Vidalia Onion, chopped

Beat cream cheese until smooth, add other ingredients. Serve with crackers. Can serve hot at 325⁰ F. in oven for 20 minutes or serve cold.

CANAPÉS

1 5-oz. jar Whiz Cheeze Spread
1 cup sifted all-purpose flour
½ cup chopped onion
4 tbsps. butter

Have cheese spread and butter at room temperature for at least 30 minutes. Blend all ingredients together smoothly. Form into a roll. Wrap roll in wax paper. Refrigerate 1 hour or longer. Preheat oven to 350⁰ F. Slice roll onto lightly floured baking sheet. Bake slices 20 minutes, or until puffed and browned. Serve hot. Approximately 24 servings.

MUSTARD ONION/SAUCE

½ cup brown mustard
1 tbsp. mayonnaise
2 tsps. sour cream
1 small onion, diced
½ tsp. paprika
$1/_{16}$ tsp. curry powder
½ tsp. parsley

Mix all ingredients together and serve with meat appetizers. Can be heated and served hot.

ONION SOUP WITH WINE

6 tbsps. butter
5 large onions,, chopped fine
3 cups chicken broth
1 cup dry white wine
1 tsp. salt
½ tsp. freshly ground pepper
¼ tsp. paprika
1 cup croutons
1 cup grated mild Cheddar cheese

Saute' onions in butter. Add chicken broth and wine, simmer for 15 to 20 minutes. Add seasonings. Garnish with croutons and cheese. Serve immediately. Serves 6.

OYSTER STEW FOR ONE

½ Vidalia Onion chopped and broiled in 2 tsps. butter until clear. Add 2 tsps. flour, ½ pt. oysters, cooked about 2 minutes, 1 cup milk, pinch of Terragon, salt and pepper. Heat about 3 to 4 minutes or until a little thick.

Jean Tollison

CHEESE ONION DIP

1 8-oz. pkg. cream cheese
1 6-oz. pkg. smoked cheese, grated
1 medium Vidalia Onion, chopped
⅓ cup pineapple juice
¼ tsp. hot sauce
1 tsp. soy sauce
1 tbsp. olives, chopped, black
1 tbps. olives, chopped, green
1 tbps. sour cream

Beat cream cheese until creamy and smooth. Add other ingredients and mix well. Chill. Use with potato chips, fritos, crackers, or strips of toasted bread.

ONION SOUP

2 tbsps. oil or margarine
1½ cups thinly sliced onions
6 cups beef broth
Black pepper
Parmesan cheese
6 sliced French bread, toasted

Saute' onions in oil until transparent and thoroughly cooked. Add broth and black pepper. Simmer 30 minutes.

Divide into 6 overproof casseroles or bowls. Top each with a slice of toasted French bread; sprinkle with parmesan cheese. Place in oven or under broiler until cheese is melted. Serve immediately. Yield: 6 servings.

Mrs. Robert P. Thompson

————— • —————

CREAM OF VIDALIA ONION SOUP

6 tbsps. margarine
4 tbsps. flour
4 cups milk
2 cups chicken stock
1 cup chopped onions
½ tsp. salt
¼ tsp. pepper
¼ cup finely cut green onions
4 tbsps. cream

Melt 2 tbsps. margarine in top of double boiler. Add flour and mix well. Add milk and chicken stock. Beat with wire whip to blend together and keep smooth. Saute' onions in 4 tbsps. margarine 3 minutes. Add to soup mixture and cook 15 minutes. Add salt, pepper, green onions, and cream. Stir to blend and serve.   Laurie & Harold Hodges

LIVER PATE

1 tsp. rendered chicken fat
2 lbs. chicken livers
⅓ cup cognac
3 eggs
1½ cups cream
⅔ cup diced chicken fat
2 medium Vidalia Onions, chopped
½ cup flour
4 tsps. salt
1 tsp. ginger
2 tsps. white pepper
1 tsp. allspice
⅛ tsp. cinnamon

Grease a 3 qt. mold. Blend livers, cognac, eggs, and cream to a fine puree, adding diced fat, onion and flour. To this mixture add all seasonings and pour into mold and cover with aluminum foil. Place in a pan of water and bake at 325⁰ F. for 2-2½ hours. Cool and store in refrigerator.

————— • —————

FIESTA ONION DIP

1 jumbo or 2 medium Vidalia Onions, chopped (with green tops, if in season)
3 tbsps. sliced black olives
3 tbsps. chopped green chili peppers
1 large or 2 medium tomatoes, (peeled or chopped)
3 tbsps. olive oil
1½ tsps. wine vinegar
⅛ tsp. cumin
Dash of Worcestershire Sauce
Dash of Tabasco Sauce
Salt and pepper to taste

Combine the above ingredients and chill well. Serve with corn chips.

Hope Manuel

Salads & Salad Dressings

SALADS

Many families do not consider a meal complete without a salad. Salads offer a variety of food value, good taste, color and delicous flavor.

There are light salads and rich, hearty molded salads, meat salads, vegetable salads and many other combinations of vegetables with protein-rich foods.

KEEP HOT SALADS HOT, AND COLD SALADS COLD.

Use variety and garnishes to make all salads attractive.

SALAD DRESSINGS

The three types of common dressings are French Dressing, Mayonnaise and cooked dressing. Salad dressings tend to make your salad complete and there are endless varieties used. Salad dressings could be thought of as a "magical act", since their contrasting colors and flavors add sparkle and refreshment to any salad.

STUFFED ONION SALAD

4-6 large Vidalia Onions
1 8-oz. pkg. cream cheese
2 tbsps. deviled ham
1 tsp. salt
Few grains pepper

Peel onions. With apple corer, remove centers of onions for use in other dishes. Beat cream cheese until soft and creamy. Blend in deviled ham and remaining ingredients. Fill center of onions with mixture and chill several hours or until cheese centers are firm. To serve, slice onions and serve on lettuce leaves. Serves 6-8.

ONION SALAD

3 cups thinly sliced Vidalia Onions
1 large head lettuce
(torn in bite size pieces)
8 hard-boiled eggs, sliced
DRESSING:
½ cup mustard
½ cup mayonnaise
Onion salt to taste
⅛ tsp. lemon pepper
2 tsps. white vinegar

Mix all dressing ingredients together. Make layers of salad by starting with ½ lettuce, ½ onion and ½ eggs. Pour ½ dressing over the combination. Repeat layers. Use remaining sauce on top. Cover and chill for 2 hours. This is very good with steak and baked potatoes.

PEPPER AND ONION 24-HOUR SALAD

2 large bell peppers, seeded and
   sliced thin
2 large Vidalia Onions, sliced
1 can shredded sauerkraut, well drained
¾ cup cider vinegar
½ cup sugar
¼ cup chopped pimento

Layer sauerkraut, onions and bell pepper in a large dish with cover. Sprinkle pimentos on top. Sprinkle sugar over top. Pour vinegar over top. DO NOT STIR. Cover. Place in refrigerator for 24-hours. Good served with pork or Saturday night hotdogs as relish.

———— • ————

VEGETABLE SALAD

1 No. 303 can small whole beets
½ cup French Dressing
4 heads Belgian Endive
2 medium Vidalia Onions, sliced
¼ tsp. paprika
½ tsp. salt
¼ tsp. coarse ground pepper
4 mushrooms
4 sprigs parsley

Drain beets. Slice and pour French Dressing over. Chill in covered bowl until very cold. To serve, wash chilled endive. Cut branches lengthwise in halves. Place 2 halves on each salad plate. Spoon generous amount of sliced beets across heavy end of stalks. Place sliced onion on top and season with salt and pepper. Can also garnish with a whole mushroom, paprika and parsley. 4 servings.

SHRIMP ONION MOLD

1 lb. shrimp, cooked and deveined
1 envelope unflavored gelatin
1 8-oz. pkg. cream cheese
1 medium Vidalia Onion, chopped
¼ tsp. lemon juice
1 cup water
½ cup mayonnaise
Food coloring if desired, red

Beat cream cheese. Dissolve gelatin in boiling water and add slowly to cream cheese mixture. Add other ingredients. Pour into mold. Chill. Serve with crackers. Prepare day before serving.

———— • ————

DELICIOUS SALAD DRESSING

1 cup mayonnaise
1 tsp. mustard
3 tbsps. chopped onions
1 tsp. paprika
1 tbsp. chopped parsley
½ tsp. salt
1 tsp. pepper, coarse, black

Mix all ingredients together and store in refrigerator. Prepare ahead and serve with shredded cabbage or lettuce. Makes 1½ cups.

TUNA SALAD SUPREME

2½ cups tuna, drained
½ cup finely chopped celery
½ cup finely chopped onions
½ cup cashews
1 tbsp. parsley, chopped
½ tsp. salt
3 hard cooked eggs
¾ to 1 cup mayonnaise
dash of pepper

Toss all together and serve on lettuce. Garnish with parsley, tomato cubes, and crackers. Use for a cold food plate.

SHRIMP AND ONION COLLAGE

1 8-oz. pkg. cream cheese
½ cup mayonnaise
2 tsps. mustard
1 tsp. salt
dash of pepper, black, coarse
1 tsp. sugar
12 oz. shrimp, cooked
3 medium onions, sliced, use tops
  for color also
3 tbsps. butter

Beat cream cheese until smooth. Add mayonnaise, mustard, salt, pepper and sugar. Fold in shrimp. Saute' onions in butter, leave crunchy. Arrange onions in salad bowl, mound shrimp in center and sprinkle with green onions. Serve with crackers.

TURKEY SALAD

3 cups cooked, diced turkey
1 can sliced, drained water chestnuts
½ cup bell pepper, diced
4 radishes, diced
¾ cup onions, diced
½ cup celery, diced
½ cup almonds, slivered
1 cup mayonnaise
1 tsp. lemon juice
1 tsp. parsley, chopped
½ tsp. curry powder

Mix all ingredients together and serve on greenest part of lettuce. Garnish with olives and serve with crackers or a congealed salad and Swiss cheese.

CARROT/ONION SALAD

6 medium carrots, cleaned
  peeled and grated
½ head of cabbage, cleaned and shredded
1 medium onion, chopped
½ to 1 cup mayonnaise
½ tsp. salt
½ tsp. pepper

Mix all together and serve on lettuce. Garnish with parsley and paprika if desired. Can add more mayonnaise, salt or pepper if desired.

MARINATED VEGETABLE SALAD

1 bunch broccoli, flowers only
1 large head cauliflower, flowers only
6 ribs celery, diced
5 large carrots, diced
2 large peppers - 1-inch sqaure pieces
2 4-oz. cans pitted ripe olives, drained
1 small pkg. radishes, diced
2 8¾-oz. cans garbanzo beans, drained
1 large bottle Italian Dressing

Mix all together and marinate in Italian Dressing. 20 servings.

COLE SLAW

½ small head white cabbage, shredded
½ small head purple cabbage, shredded
1 medium onion, chopped
2 tsps. salt
½ cup salad oil
½ cup sugar
¾ cup white vinegar

Mix all ingredients together. Cover and refrigerate overnight. Serve cold on a bed of parsley or lettuce with whole mushrooms, cauliflower or broccoli flowerets.

ONION SALAD

3 large Vidalia Onions, peeled & sliced
2 large green peppers, sliced
1 large red pepper, sliced
1 head crisp Romaine lettuce
Italian or herb dressing

Arrange equal amounts of peppers and onions on Romaine lettuce and garnish with 1 whole mushroom and parsley sprigs. An Herb Dressing or Italian Dressing shows colors better.

———— • ————

TOSSED GREEN SALAD

1 head curly endive, cleaned and broken up in bite-size pieces
1 head escarole, cleaned and broken up in bite-size pieces
2 tomatoes, wedged
Salt
10 small ripe olives
½ bunch broccoli, cleaned, washed, use tops only
2 tbsps. wine vinegar
¼ cup olive oil
Freshly ground black pepper, coarse

Toss greens in with all ingredients. Serve immediately.

SALAD

2 cups celery strips
3 canned pimentos
Catalina Dressing
2 green peppers, whole
1 medium onion, chopped
Lettuce

Cut the celery into short, thin strips. Cover the peppers with boiling water, let stand 5 minutes, remove dry & chill, then cut in strips the same size as celery. Rinse the pimentos in cold water. Dry and cut in same size as celery. Mix with Catalina Dressing and serve in nests of lettuce. Serves 6.

STUFFED CELERY SALAD

1 small stalk celery
8 oz. cream cheese, softened
1 small onion, chopped
French Dressing
1 head lettuce
1 tsp. evaporated milk
1 tbsp. chives

Beat cream cheese until smooth. Add milk, onion, and chives. Fill the celery with the cheese filling. Cut into 1-inch pieces and serve on lettuce with French Dressing. Serve 6

CABBAGE SALAD

1 cup shredded cabbage, white
1 medium onion, choppped
1 tsp. sour cream
½ tsp. coarsely ground pepper
1 cup shredded cabbage, purple
¼ cup mayonnaise
1 tsp. salt
Romaine Lettuce

Mix together and serve on Romaine lettuce. Garnish with freshly cut vegetables. Serves 4.

———— • ————

HOT ONION SALAD

1 red pepper, cut in thin strips
1 medium onion, sliced
1 lb. fresh mushrooms, sliced
1 can water chestnuts, drained
1 tbsp. margarine or butter
1 tbsp. soy sauce
LETTUCE:
4 slices bacon, crumbled
2 tbsps. grated mild American cheese

Combine all ingredients (except lettuce, bacon and cheese) in a skillet. Saute' until tender. Spoon over lettuce and garnish with bacon and cheese. 4 servings.

MARINATED VEGETABLES

3 medium onions, sliced
½ cauliflower, flowered
½ bunch broccoli, use tops only with flowers
10 radishes, sliced
1 rib celery, diced
2 medium cucumbers, diced
1 medium carrot, diced
½ tsp. salt
1 bottle Wish Bone Italian Dressing

Clean all vegetables and marinate in Wish Bone Italian Dressing.

BACON & ONION SALAD

2 large or 3 medium heads Romaine lettuce
5 green onions, minced
½ tsp. freshly ground pepper
6 hard cooked eggs
¾ lb. bacon
3 tbsps. vinegar
½ tsp. salt, as desired

Wash and crisp the Romaine lettuce. Chop the eggs. Cook bacon until crisp, then drain and crumble. Save fat. Break lettuce into a bowl, sprinkle with the chopped eggs, onions and bacon. Heat the bacon fat and add the vinegar, salt and pepper. Pour over salad and mix thoroughly. Taste for seasonings and add more salt if necessary. Mix again immediately before serving. Serves 12.

TUNA SALAD

6-oz. can tuna, packed in oil
1 small onion, chopped
1 tsp. mustard
1 tbsp. mayonnaise
2 tbsps. minced parsley
4 hard-boiled eggs, chopped

Drain tuna; add other ingredients, toss lightly. Chill several hours before serving. Serve on greens and garnish with egg slices, pimento or fresh mushroom slices. Serves 2.

LOBSTER SALAD

2 2-lb. live lobsters
4 tbsps. Amontillado sherry
4 tbsps. minced parsley
2 tbsps. olive oil
2 small onions, sliced

Cook lobster and remove meat. Add remaining ingredients and toss lightly. Chill several hours before serving. Serve on Romaine Lettuce. Serves 4.

• Refer to Lobster Casserole for directions on cooking lobster. (Entrees)

VIDALIA ONION SALAD

3 large Vidalia Onions, sliced
1 cup white vinegar
½ cup water
¾ cup sugar
1 tsp. salt
1 tsp. parsley, chopped
⅛ tsp. basil
dash or red pepper

Combine all ingredients except onions and heat until sugar melts. Pour over onions and serve over lettuce. Keeps well refrigerated for several days if stored in an air-tight container.

SHRIMP SALAD

1 pt. shrimp, cleaned, deveined & peeled
6 green peppers
1 medium onion, diced
Mayonnaise
paprika
1 small bottle stuffed olives
12 small sweet pickles
Romaine lettuce
Catalina Dressing
Sour Cream

Chop shrimp into bite-size pieces and dress with Catalina Dressing. Chill for 2 hours. Add olives, sweet pickles and onions. Hollow out green peppers to form cups and stuff with this mixture. Mix mayonnaise and sour cream together. Serve garnished with lettuce, mayonnaise and sour cream. Sprinkle with paprika.

———— • ————

STUFFED ONION SALAD

4 to 6 Large Vidalia Onions
1 8-oz. pkg. cream cheese
2 tbsps. deviled ham
1 tsp. dry mustard
1 tbsp. chopped pimento
¼ tsp. salt and few grains pepper

Peel onions. With apple corer remove center of onions and reserve these portions for use in other dishes. Beat cream cheese until soft and creamy. Blend in deviled ham and remaining ingredients. Fill centers on onions with mixture and chill several hours or until cheese centers are firm. To serve, slice onions and place on lettuce leaves. Serves 6 to 8.

VIDALIA ONION MUSTARD SAUCE

2 tbsps. butter, margarine or salad oil
1 cup sour cream
1 tbsp. prepared mustard
½ cup minced onions
½ tbsp. salt
⅛ tsp. red pepper
1 tbsp. chopped scallions

Combine butter, cream, mustard, onion, salt and pepper. Heat over low heat. Sprinkle with scallion. Serve on grilled franks, hamburgers, luncheon meat, fish, chicken, etc. Makes about 1 cup.

MUSHROOM/ONION SALAD

1½ cups sliced watercress
2 cups sliced mushrooms, fresh
1/3 cup French Dressing
2 cups sliced Vidalia Onions
½ cup sliced radishes

Arrange watercress in the center of a bowl. Cover with onions, mushrooms, and radishes. Mix together. Pour dressing over vegetables. Serves 6.

———— • ————

DRESSING

1½ cups mayonnaise
¼ cup chili sauce
1/3 cup whipped cream
1 medium onion, chopped
3 tbsps. finely chopped parsley

Mix mayonnaise, onion and parsley. Chill 1 hour. Fold in whipped cream and top salad with chili sauce. Serves 4 to 6.

CARROT/ONION SLAW

6 medium carrots
¾ cup diced celery
½ cup diced Vidalia Onions
⅓ cup raisins
½ cup diced apple
½ cup diced green or red pepper
¾ cup mayonnaise
Salt
Freshly ground pepper

Grate carrots. Toss with celery, onions, raisins, apple and peppers. Mix in mayonnaise and season with salt and pepper. Chill thoroughly.

RICE SALAD
WITH PEAS & ONIONS

1½ cups long-grain rice
1 pkg. frozen peas, cooked
2 tbsps. margarine
¾ cup French Dressing
3 medium Vidalia Onions, chopped

Pour 2 qts. water into a saucepan and bring to a rolling boil. Add the rice slowly and cook for 14 minutes, or until tender, but still firm. Drain thoroughly. Add the salad dressing and the peas. Saute' onions in margarine and fold into rice mixture. Pack the rice in a mold and let chill. At serving time, unmold onto a platter and arrange pimento or eggs in a pattern over the dome of rice. Serves 8.

TUNA ONION SALAD

6-oz. can tuna, drained
1 medium onion, chopped
2 tbsps. minced parsley
1 tbps. mayonnaise
¼ cup slivered almonds

Mix tuna, mayonnaise, onions, and almonds. Chill several hours before serving. Serve on greens and garnish with parsley. Serves 2.

LENTIL SALAD

1 cup lentils
1½ tsps. salt
3 tbsps. oil
1 tbsp. vinegar
1 medium onion, minced
Freshly ground pepper
¼ tsp. dry mustard
1 tbsp. minced parsley

Simmer lentils in 3 cups water with 1 tsp. salt 35 minutes, until tender. Drain. In a small bowl, mix oil, vinegar, onion, pepper and mustard. Toss with lentils while they are hot. Refrigerate and, when cool, mix in the parsley and salt to taste.

WILD RICE/OYSTER/
ONION CASSEROLE

½ cup butter
¾ cup celery or bell pepper
3 cups cooked wild rice
Half & Half
¼ tsp. pepper, black coarse, ground
¾ cup chopped Vidalia Onions
¼ cup water chestnuts
1 pt. oysters with liquor
1 tsp. salt
¼ tsp. caraway seeds
1 cup grated Cheddar cheese

Heat ¼ cup butter in a skillet and cook the onions and celery, or bell pepper, until soft and barely golden. Combine with the rice. Grease casserole dish and add water chestnuts, drained oysters, reserving liquor. Mix oyster liquor and Half & Half to make ¾ cup. Add salt, pepper, caraway seeds and milk with oyster liquor and pour it over mixture in casserole. Top with grated cheese. Melt in remaining ¼ cup butter and sprinkle with cheese. Bake covered, in preheated 350⁰ F. oven for 30 minutes. Serves 4.

MUSHROOM ONION SALAD

3 medium onions, sliced
1 bunch Pascal celery
3 tbsps. olive oil
1 tsp. salt
1 head Bibb or Romaine lettuce
1½ lbs. mushrooms
2½ tbsps. minced chives
1 tbsps. tarragon vinegar
½ tsp. freshly ground pepper

Peel and slice the onions. Rinse the raw mushrooms and dry them. Slice the stems and cut the caps into cubes or pie-shaped wedges. Cube the inner stalks of the bunch of Pascal celery. Combine mushrooms and celery with minced chives and marinate the mixture in a dressing made with the olive oil, tarragon vinegar, salt and pepper. Chill for 30 minutes. When ready to serve, lift salad out of the dressing and pile it on Bibb or Romaine lettuce leaves. Dust with the freshly ground pepper. Garnish with hard boiled eggs, parsley, pimento, or strips of bacon. Serve with pork chops, steak or lamb.

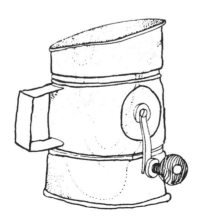

TOMATO/ONION SALAD

6 large Vidalia Onions, sliced
2 tsps. fresh basil or 1 tsp. dried basil
6 tbsps. olive oil
2 tbsps. chopped parsley
6 large ripe tomatoes
1 tsp. salt
1 tsp. freshly ground pepper
¼ cup cognac

Peel and slice the onions. Scald, peel and chill the tomatoes. Cut them in paper thin slices and arrange overlapping on a dish alternating tomatoes and onion slices. Pour over them a mixture of the basil, salt, pepper, olive oil and cognac. Sprinkle with finely chopped parsley and chill before serving. Serves 6.

Breads, Pastas, Rice

Breads are good sources of iron and are among the best sources of Thiamin. The whole grain bran and germ products have more fiber than refined flours.

Breads appear on the tables of many homes at every meal.

Some popular pasta products include spaghetti, noodles and macaroni. These come in a wide variety of shapes.

For many people rice is the staff of life. Half of the people in the world derive at least sixty percent of their energy from rice.

———— • ————

ONIONS WITH RICE

1½ cups long grain rice
2 qts. boiling water
1 tsp. salt
¼ cup butter or margarine
2 tbsps. grated Parmesan cheese
4 cups thinly sliced Vidalia Onions
   (about 3)
½ tsp. salt
⅛ tsp. paprika

Drop rice into rapidly boiling water with 1 tsp. salt added. Boil uncovered about 5 minutes. Drain at once. Melt butter in 2 qt. casserole in oven, stir in onions. Add ½ tsp. salt and stir onions in butter until they are yellowed and coated. Then add rice and stir to distribute evenly. Cover and bake in slow oven at 325⁰ F. for 1 hour. Sprinkle with paprika and cheese. Serves 8.

———— • ————

ONION FRIED RICE

8 strips bacon
1 bunch Vidalia Onions, green or
   1 large Vidalia Onion
3 eggs well beaten
1 lb. fresh mushrooms, sliced or
   1 large can, drained and sliced
2½ cups cooked day old rice
¼ cup soy sauce, Japanese
1 can water chestnuts, sliced & drained
Leftover chicken, pork, shrimp or cheese

Cook bacon in wok or fryer until crisp. Drain on paper towels and crumble, leaving bacon grease in pan. Saute' onions in grease over medium heat until tender. Add eggs, scramble until done and crumble. Add rice; stir to combine. Add bacon, water chestnuts, mushrooms, and chopped meat if desired. Sprinkle with soy sauce to taste and stir over low heat until mixture is thoroughly combined and warm.

ONION CHEESE LOAF

Cut French bread loaf in 1-inch slices cutting to but not through bottom of loaf. Combine ⅓ cup butter, softened, and 3 tbsps. prepared mustard; spread over cut surfaces of bread. Insert slices of sharp process American cheese and then slices of Vidalia Sweet Onions in slashes. Wrap loaf in foil; heat over medium coals about 15 minutes or until hot.

———— • ————

ONION MUFFINS

2 cups sifted flour
3 tsps. baking powder
½ tsp. salt
2 tbsps. sugar
1 egg
1 cup whole milk
2 tbsps. melted shortening
½ cup Vidalia Onions, chopped
2 tbsps. butter

Saute' onions in butter, until translucent. Sift together flour, baking powder, salt and sugar. Beat egg and add milk and melted shortening. Add egg mixture to flour mixture, stirring only until flour is moistened. Add onions. Fill greased muffin tins ½ to ⅔ full and bake in moderately hot oven, 425⁰ F. for 20 minutes.

ONION BREAD

1 loaf French Bread
1 small Vidalia Onion, chopped
1 tsp. onion salt
4 tbsps. margarine

Saute' onions in margarine until translucent. Mix with salt and spread over French bread. Serve hot.

PIZZA WITH ONIONS

CRUST: Grease pan and sprinkle with 2 tbsps. yellow cornmeal. Mix 2 cups packaged Bisquick mix and ½ cup water together with a fork and knead 6 to 10 times. Roll and line pizza pan, crimping edges. Bake at 425⁰ F. for 12 minutes or until golden brown.
FILLING: ½ lb. ground beef
½ cup chopped onions
¼ cup bell peppers, red, diced
1 cup mild American cheese
½ cup Caraway Seed cheese
⅛ tsp. basil
1 small can tomato paste
½ cup mushrooms, sliced
¼ cup celery, diced
¼ cup Monterey Jack or Swiss cheese
⅛ tsp. oregano
⅛ tsp. garlic salt

Saute' all ingredients together except cheese and mushrooms. Pour over crust. Cook for about 20-30 minutes or until both crust and filling is hot and bubbly. Let stand 3 minutes before serving. Delicious!

RICE WITH ONIONS

½ cup melted butter
3 eggs, beaten
1 cup rice, minute, cooked
1 cup diced tomatoes
¼ tsp. salt, optional
1 large chopped Vidalia Onion
1½ cups milk
1 lb. Cheddar cheese, grated
½ tsp. salt, optional

Brown onions in butter. Mix remaining ingredients together. Add onions. Mix well. Place in ungreased baking sheet. Bake 45 minutes at 350⁰ F. 6 to 8 servings.

ONION BISCUITS

3 cups flour
2 tsps. salt
½ qt. milk
¼ cup baking powder
½ cup shortening
½ cup chopped Vidalia Onions

Mix and sift the dry ingredients and with a fork cut in shortening. Gradually add milk and onions until a soft dough is created. Amount of milk may vary with the different flours. Roll into biscuits and place in a greased pan. Makes about 25 small biscuits.

————— • —————

CORN BREAD

3 medium Vidalia Onions, diced
3 eggs
2 17-oz. cans cream style corn
¾ cup sour cream
6 tbsps. butter or mayonnaise
2 tbsps. evaporated milk
1 pkg. cornmeal muffin mix
2½ cups sharp Cheddar cheese, grated
  (10 oz.)

Preheat oven to 425° F. Butter 13" x 9" baking pan. Saute' onions in mayonnaise or butter until translucent. Blend eggs, milk and corn muffin mix. Place in casserole dish. Top with onions, spread with sour cream and sprinkle with cheese. Bake 40 minutes until golden brown. Let stand 10 minutes before cutting.

YEAST ONION SANDWICHES

1 loaf yeast bread
48 thin slices Vidalia Onions
pepper
mayonnaise
salt
parsley

Cut yeast bread in 24 slices, should make 48 small round sandwiches. Cut 4 rounds from each slice of bread. Mix mayonnaise, salt, pepper and 2 tbsps. parsley, and spread generously on bread. Place 1 slice of onion on top. Roll edges in mayonnaise and then in parsley. Press sandwiches together firmly. Wrap in foil and refrigerate until thoroughly chilled.

————— • —————

CHICKEN/ONION SANDWICH

1 medium Vidalia Onion, chopped
2 slices rye bread
¼ tsp. caraway seeds
salt to taste
1 tsp. butter
3 oz. cream cheese
2 slices white chicken meat
pepper to paste

Beat butter and cream cheese until smooth. Add onions, caraway seeds, salt and pepper. Spread mixture on rye bread and place 1 slice chicken on bread and spread with cream cheese. Top with other slice of chicken and spread cream cheese mixture on other slice of bread. Delicious!

ONION CORN STICKS

3 tbsps. margarine
¾ cup sifted all-purpose flour
1 tsp. salt
2 eggs
4 tbsps. shortening
1 medium Vidalia Onion, chopped
1 cup yellow cornmeal
3 tsps. baking powder
1 cup evaporated milk
1 tsp. sugar

Saute' onions in butter. Sift dry ingredients together. Preheat oven to 400° F. Combine eggs, milk, sugar, and shortening. Blend 15 seconds or until smooth. Pour over dry ingredients and stir lightly, just enought to combine ingredients. Bake 20 to 25 minutes. Makes 12 corn sticks.

ONION NUT BREAD

3 cups sifted all-purpose flour
½ cup sugar
½ cup chopped onions
2 eggs
½ cup butter, melted
4½ tsps. baking powder
1 tsp. salt
¾ cup chopped walnuts
1 cup milk

Saute' onions in ¼ cup butter until translucent. Sift the flour, baking powder, sugar, and salt together in a mixing bowl. Then stir in onions and nuts. Beat the egg, milk and ¼ cup melted butter. Add to the flour mixture and stir until very well mixed, but don't attempt to beat out all the lumps. Spoon into greased a loaf pan and bake in preheated 350° F. oven for 1 hour. Turn out of pan and cool before serving.

STUFFED MANICOTTI FOR TWO

4 manicotti shells
3 qts. boiling water
Salt
½ lb. ground chuck
1 medium Vidalia Onion, finely chopped
½ green pepper, finely chopped
1 15-oz. can tomato sauce
2 tsps. oregano
1 tsp. thyme
1 bay leaf
1 cup shredded Mozzarella cheese, divided

Cook manicotti shells in boiling, salted water for 10 minutes; drain. Rinse in cold water; drain and set aside. Saute' ground chuck, onion and green pepper until brown; drain. Add tomato sauce, oregano, thyme, and bay leaf; simmer over low heat 10 minutes. Add ½ cup cheese, stirring until melted. Arrange manicotti shells in a shallow dish; stuff with ½ of meat mixture. Pour remaining meat mixture over shells and top with remaining ½ cup cheese. Bake at 300° F. for 30 minutes.

Marianne McMillan

ONION CHEESE SANDWICH

3 tbsps. butter
1 large onion, sliced
1 slice Mozzarella cheese
⅛ tsp. coarse black pepper
2 pieces white bread
1 slice Swiss cheese
¼ tsp. salt

Melt butter and place 1 slice of bread in skillet with 2 cheese slices, onion, salt and pepper, and top with other slice of bread. Cook as you would a grilled cheese sandwich. Cook until cheese melts brown on both sides and serve hot.

CRACKED WHEAT ONION LOAVES

½ cup fine cracked wheat
1 pkg. granular yeast
¼ cup vegetable shortening
2 tbsps. light molasses
⅔ cup milk
4 cups (approximately) all-purpose flour
1½ cups boiling water
⅔ cup warm water
2 tsps. salt
2 tbsps. honey
1 cup whole-wheat flour
½ cup onions
3 tbsps. butter

Saute' onions in butter until translucent. Cook the cracked wheat in the boiling water for 15 to 20 minutes, stirring occasionally. For the last few minutes, raise the heat and stir constantly until all the water has evaporated. Meanwhile, dissolve the yeast in warm water. Add the shortening, salt, molasses, honey, and milk to the cooked cracked wheat, stir and cool to lukewarm. Combine with the dissolved yeast, stir in the whole wheat flour and 2½ cups of the all-purpose flour. Gradually knead in as much of the remaining flour as is necessary to obtain a smooth dough that has lost most of its stickiness. (You may need to use more than 4 cups of flour, it depends on the moisture of the cooked cracked wheat.) Place the dough in a bowl, cover and let rise in a warm place for 1½ hours, or until double in bulk. Punch it down and divide into 8 equal portions. Shape each portion into a small loaf and make even diagonal slits on top with a knife. Cover and let rise 1 hour or until double in bulk. Bake in preheated 375⁰ F. oven for 35 minutes. Cool loaves on rack. These loaves may be frozen.

ONION CORN BREAD

½ cup sifted flour
1½ tsps. salt
2 tsps. double-action baking powder
⅔ cup melted butter
1½ cups cornmeal (yellow or white)
1 tsp. sugar
3 eggs, medium
1 cup Half & Half
¾ cup chopped Vidalia Onions

Saute' onions in ⅓ cup butter until translucent. Mix the dry ingredients. Beat the eggs with the cream and add them to the cornmeal mixture and add onions. Stir in the melted butter and blend thoroughly. Spread the batter in a well-buttered jelly roll tin and bake in a 400⁰ F. oven for 15 to 18 minutes, or until lightly browned and done. Cut the hot corn bread into squares and split and butter them at once.

COTTAGE CHEESE-ONION MUFFINS

2 cups all-purpose flour, sifted
2 tbsps. sugar
2 tbsps. Vidalia Onions, chopped
3 tbsps. melted butter
3 tbsps. baking soda
1 tbsp. chives
2 eggs, beaten
¾ cup milk
1 cup cottage cheese, creamed, small curd

Grease muffin tins. Preheat oven to 400⁰ F. Sift dry ingredients together and add all other ingredients by order. Fold in cottage cheese last. Fill muffin tins ½ full and bake 15 to 20 minutes. Cool a few minutes and remove from oven. Serve with butter. Serves 18 muffins.

ONION CORNBREAD

3 tbsps. butter
2 cups cornmeal, sifted, plain, white
½ cup buttermilk
1 medium Vidalia Onion, chopped
1½ tsps. salt
¾ tsp. soda
Add water - Do not get too soupy

Preheat oven to 450° F. Saute' onions in margarine. Sift dry ingredients and add milk and water. Grease pan with bacon grease and sprinkle with meal. Remove excess meal. Cook in top level of oven. Cook about 30 minutes or until brown.

ONIONS ROLLS

¼ cup butter
⅛ cup sugar
1 tbsp. honey
2 medium Vidalia Onions, sliced
2 tbsps. poppy seed
1 pkg. crescent rolls

Melt butter and saute' onions until tender. Add sugar, poppy seeds, and honey. Place spoonful of onions on each roll and roll into dough. Bake by crescent roll directions. Sprinkle with paprika when done and brush with melted margarine.

ONION MUFFINS

1 cup self-rising flour, sifted
1 tbsp. mayonnaise
½ cup milk
½ cup onions, chopped

Put all ingredients in a mixing bowl and beat until smooth. Grease muffin tins and make 8 muffins. Bake in preheated 450° F. oven for 8 to 10 minutes. Serves 8.

ONION CHEESE BISCUITS

3 tbsps. margarine
1 stick margarine, softened
1 3-oz. pkg. cream cheese, softened
¼ tsp. salt
Paprika
1 medium onion, chopped
¼ lb. cheese, softened
1 tsp. Worcestershire Sauce
1 cup flour
¼ tsp. pepper

Saute' onions in margarine. Blend margarine and cheese until smooth. Add Worcestershire sauce. Add all other ingredients and shape into balls. Place in preheated 350° oven for 20 minutes or until done. Sprinkle with paprika if desired.

———— • ————

ONION POPOVERS

3 tbsps. margarine
1 cup flour, all-purpose, sifted 2 times
2 eggs
1 medium Vidalia Onion, chopped
¾ tsp. salt
1 tbsp. shortening
1 cup evaporated milk

Saute' onions in margarine. Grease custard cups (12 medium) and place on a baking sheet. Preheat oven to 375° F. Sift dry ingredients and cut in shortening. Beat eggs and milk with beater. Add flour mixture and heat until smooth. Fill cups ⅓ full. Bake 50 minutes. Remove from oven, cut slits in sides of popovers to release steam. Return to oven for 10 minutes. Quickly remove popovers so not to become soft. Serve promptly. Serves 12.

ONION BROWN BREAD

2 cups cornmeal
2 cups rye meal
2 tsps. salt
1½ tsps. soda
½ cup molasses
½ cup honey
1 cup buttermilk
1 cup water
3 tbsps. margarine
1 medium Vidalia Onion, chopped

Saute' onions in margarine until translucent. Mix ingredients in order given. Steam in a closely covered greased tin for 3 hours. Then remove, cover and bake in a 325º F. for 30 minutes.

———— • ————

ONION MUFFINS

3 tbsps. margarine
1¾ cups sifted flour, all-purpose
½ tsp. salt
½ tsp. soda
1½ cups sour cream
1 medium Vidalia Onion, finely chopped
2 tbsps. baking powder
3 tbsps. sugar
1 egg

Saute' onions in margarine until translucent. Sift dry ingredients together. Beat egg until foamy. Add cream and mix well. Stir into dry ingredients until mixed together. Pour into muffin tin. Bake 20 minutes in 350º F. preheated oven for about 30 minutes. Makes 12 muffins.

ONION PANCAKES

3 tbsps. margarine
2 cups sifted cake flour
1 tsp. salt
1 egg
¼ cup margarine, melted
1 medium Vidalia Onion, chopped
2 tsps. baking powder
¼ cup sugar
1 cup evaporated milk

Saute' onions in butter. Sift dry ingredients. Blend egg, milk, and margarine together. Mix all ingredients together and cook on a hot griddle. Serves 12.

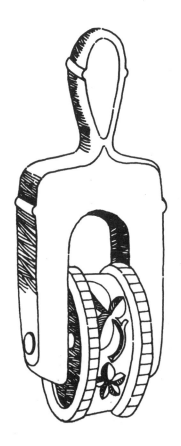

HOT BREAD

1 cup corn meal
½ cup flour
½ tsp. salt
1 cup evaporated milk
3 tbsps. plus 1 tsp. melted butter
½ cup rye meal
2 tbsps. sugar
1 tsp. soda
3 tbsps. honey or molasses
1 medium Vidalia Onion, chopped

Saute' onions in 3 tbsps. butter until translucent. Mix together dry ingredients. Add milk, molasses, butter and onions. Beat thoroughly. Place in well greased molds for 2½ hours. Bake in over at 300⁰ F. for 15 minutes.

ONION BISCUITS

2 cups sifted self-rising flour
1 cup milk
3 tbsps. margarine
2 tbsps. shortening
water as needed
1 small Vidalia Onion, chopped

Saute' onions in margarine. Sift dry ingredients together, work in shortening and add milk and water as necessary. Fold in onion. Roll in biscuits. Bake in preheated 350⁰ F. oven for 25 to 30 minutes, until brown. Brush with melted margarine before serving.

ONION BISCUITS

2 cups sifted flour
1 tsp. sugar
5 tbsps. butter
1½ cup Vidalia Onions, chopped
3½ tsps. baking powder
1 tsp. salt
1½ tbsps. lard
½ cup evaporated milk

Mix dry ingredients together. Mix in shortening. Saute' onions in 3 tbsps. margarine until translucent. Add onions to shortening and milk. Pat and roll on floured board. Shape with biscuit cutter and place in greased pan. Bake in hot oven for 15 minutes at 400⁰ F.

———— • ————

ONION SPOON BREAD

1 medium Vidalia Onion, chopped
2 cups milk, evaporated
1 qt. boiling water
1 cup cornmeal
1 lb. bacon
3 tbsps. margarine
2 eggs, beaten
1 tsp. salt
2 cups boiled rice

Saute' onions in margarine. Scald milk in double boiler and pour on beaten eggs. Return to boiler and cook until it covers the spoon. Add salt to boiling water. Stir in cornmeal and cook 5 minutes. Place in a buttered baking dish and add alternately spoonfuls of mush and rice until baking dish is full. Arrange bacon across top of dish. Bake in moderate oven for 40 minutes at 350⁰ F. If excess grease develops, drain before serving.

Entrees

MEAT / EGGS

Meat has long had an important role in our diet. Meat and eggs are good sources of protein and also sources of iron, zinc, Vitamin B[12] and Vitamin B complex.

Cholesterol is of animal origin. Whether you are planning an elegant sit-down dinner or an informal picnic, meat is always at its versatile best. Preparation is as simple as broiling, boiling, baking, roasting, stewing and frying.

———— • ————

SWISS ONION BAKE

2 tbsps. butter
2 cups sliced Vidalia Onions
6 hard-cooked eggs, sliced
6 oz. process Swiss cheese, shredded
1 1½-oz. can condensed cream of
   chicken soup
¾ cup milk
½ tsp. prepared mustard
6 slices French bread

In a skillet, melt butter; add sliced onions and cook till tender. Spread in bottom of 10 x 6 x 1½-inch baking dish. Top onion with eggs, sliced; sprinkle with shredded Swiss cheese. Mix can of soup, milk and mustard; heat, stirring till smooth. Pour sauce over casserole, being sure some goes to the bottom. Place bread, cut ½-inch thick and buttered, on top, overlapping a little. Bake at 350⁰ F. for 35 minutes or till hot. Broil a few minutes to toast bread. Serves 6.

———— • ————

ZWIEBEL KUCHEN (GERMAN ONION PIE)

Pastry for baked 10" pie shell
1½ cups sifted flour
¾ tsp. salt
1½ tsps. caraway seeds
½ cup shortening
2-3 tbsps. water
3 cups thinly sliced Vidalia Onions
3 tbsps. melted butter, margarine or fat
½ cup milk
1½ cups dairy sour cream
1 tsp. salt
2 eggs, well beaten
3 tbsps. flour
bacon slices

Combine flour, salt and caraway seeds. Add shortening; cut into flour until mixture adheres and follows fork around bowl. Turn onto floured board; roll to ⅛ inch thickness. Fit into 10-inch pie pan. Bake in hot oven (425⁰ F) 10 minutes, or until lightly browned. Cook onions in fat until lightly browned. Spoon onto pastry shell. Add milk, 1¼ cup sour cream, and salt to eggs. Blend flour with ¼ cup sour cream. Combine with egg mixture; pour over onion mixture. Bake in slow oven (325⁰ F) 30 minutes, or until firm in center. Garnish with slices of crisp-fried bacon. Makes 8 servings.

———— • ————

SAUSAGE ONION QUICHE

1 pie shell, unbaked
½ cup chopped onion
½ cup sour cream
1 cup Caraway Seed cheese, grated
2 tbsps. parsley
½ lb. hot sausage
2 eggs, beaten
1 cup Monterey Jack cheese, grated
¾ cup grated Cheddar cheese
salt and pepper to taste

Cook sausage and onions, drain. Mix other ingredients, except cheddar cheese, together and put in pie shell. Garnish with cheddar cheese and parsley. Bake at 350⁰ F for 35 to 40 minutes.

BASEL ONION TART

Dough:
2 cups all-purpose flour
½ tsp. salt
½ cup butter
4 tbsps. ice water

1½ tbsps. butter
6 large Vidalia Onions, thinly sliced
½ tsp. salt
⅓ cup diced bacon
2 cups milk
3 tbsps. all-purpose flour
2 eggs, well beaten
2 cups shredded cheese

To make dough, sift flour with salt. Cut in butter until particles are the size of small peas. Add ice water. Stir until a stiff dough is formed. Knead on a lightly floured board. Roll out to fit the bottom and sides of a well-buttered 10" layer cake pan. Prick several times with a fork. To make filling, heat butter in a pan and saute' onions. Add salt and diced bacon. Cook over medium heat until onions and and bacon are golden brown. Add milk gradually to the flour. Stir until smooth. Beat in eggs and cheese. Add saute'ed onions and bacon, including the fat in which they were saute'ed. Pour mixture into dough-lined pan. Bake at 350⁰ F for 30 minutes. Raise oven temperature to 400⁰ F and bake 5 minutes or longer or until top is browned and crisp. Cut into wedges; serve hot. Serves 6.

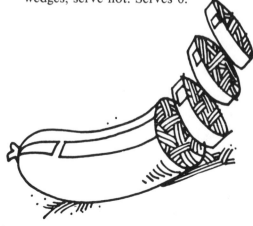

ONION SAUCE

10 medium Vidalia Onions,
  peeled & diced fine
¼ tsp. pepper
1 tbsp. soy sauce
¼ cup butter
½ tsp. salt
¼ tsp. oregano
½ cup hot water

Cook onions in butter until translucent. Add salt, pepper and oregano. Mix well. Pour mixture into glass container, add hot water and cover. Blend until onions are minced (approximately 3 seconds). Reheat and serve hot. Serve on steaks, hamburgers, liver, or any meats.

BAR-B-QUE SAUCE

1 pt. vinegar
1 tbsp. black pepper, coarse
1 tsp. salt
1 cup catsup
1 cup oil, salad
1 tbsp. poultry seasoning
½ stick butter
½ cup Vidalia Onions, chopped

Mix together ingredients in saucepan and heat. Baste chicken while on grill. Makes enough to baste 5 chickens. Refrigerate in air-tight container.

SCRAMBLED CHEESE EGGS WITH ONIONS

2 tbsps. margarine
½ cup mild American cheese, grated
3 eggs, whole and beat
½ cup chopped Vidalia Onions

Melt margarine. Add onions and saute'. Mix cheese and eggs together and add to onion mixture. Cook until done. Serve hot.

SAUCE FOR HAM

1 tbsp. oil
¼ cup dark brown sugar
2 tbsps. vinegar
1 medium Vidalia Onion, chopped
1 tbsp. mustard, prepared
5 tbsps. catsup
1 tsp. lemon juice

Mix all ingredients together and simmer until well blended. May be prepared 1 or 2 days in advance. Fabulous on sliced ham.
1½ cups.

———— • ————

ONION BAR-B-QUE SAUCE

1 envelope Lipton Onion Soup Mix
½ cup dark brown sugar
1 tbsp. mustard, prepared
1 small onion, chopped
1 cup chili sauce
¼ cup lemon juice
1½ cups water

Mix all ingredients together and cook for 20 minutes. Makes 2½ cups sauce.

———— • ————

SHRIMP ONION CASSEROLE

2 lbs. shrimp, boiled and hulled
1 medium Vidalia Onion, chopped
2 cups grated cheese
1 lb. fresh mushrooms
1 can cream of chicken soup
1 can French Fried Onion Rings

Mix first five ingredients and put in casserole or chafing dish. Cook at 350° F for 30 minutes and take out of oven and top with 1 can of French Fried Onion Rings. Brown. Serve hot.

ONIONS WITH SAUSAGE

4 cups sausage, ground
½ cup cream
3 cups Vidalia Onions, chopped

Mix sausage and onion. Add ½ cup cream. Form into cakes and brown on both sides in a frying pan. Serve with griddle cakes.

ESCALLOPED SALMON AND ONIONS

5 tbsps. butter
1½ cups milk
1 No. 1 can salmon, remove bones
1 cup onion, chopped
3 tbsps. flour
⅛ tsp. salt
1 cup dry bread crumbs

Use 2 tbsps. butter and saute' onions until translucent. Blend flour in. Add milk and cook over low heat until smooth and thickened. Add salmon. Arrange in greased baking dish in alternate layers with bread crumbs, beginning with salmon mixture and having crumbs on top. Bake in 375⁰ F. oven, 35 to 40 minutes.

HAM ONION CASSEROLE

1 cup Vidalia Onions, chopped
4 cups ham, diced
1 or 2 tsp. bacon fat
1 egg
⅛ tsp. pepper

Combine the ham and onions and mix the egg and pepper into a mixture. Form into small cakes and brown on both sides in a frying pan containing a little bacon fat.

LOBSTER ONION SALAD

4 lobsters, cooked & shelled, meat only
2 tbsps. vinegar
4 medium Vidalia Onions, sliced
1 small bottle Catalina dressing

Mix together and serve on lettuce with crackers and fresh fruit. Drain, if need before place on lettuce. Let marinate overnight before serving.

———— • ————

CHICKEN SALAD WITH VIDALIA ONIONS

3 cups diced chicken
1 medium Vidalia Onion, diced
½ tsp. salt
3 hard-boiled eggs, chopped
¼ cup diced celery
3 to 4 tbsps. mayonnaise
⅛ tsp. pepper, black, coarse

Mix all ingredients together and serve on lettuce with crackers.

———— • ————

PORK CHOPS WITH VIDALIA ONIONS

2 cups rice, uncooked
4 medium pork chops
1 lb. mushrooms, sliced, drained
1 can water chestnuts, drained
¼ cup water
2 cans cream of chicken soup
2 medium Vidalia Onions, sliced

Grease casserole pan and layer with uncooked rice and water. Add washed and cleaned pork chops. Mix other ingredients together and pour over pork chops. Cook at 350⁰ F. for 1 to 1½ hours until done.

LOBSTER CASSEROLE

2 2-lb. live lobsters
1 medium onion, chopped
1 can water chestnuts, drained
6 small green Vidalia Onions, chopped
1 can cream of chicken soup

Kill lobsters by inserting a knife in the shell where the body and the tail meet and severing the spinal cord. Flip the lobsters over on their backs and split them lengthwise. Remove sac behind eyes and intestinal vein and discard. Take meat out of shells.Cook lobster and remove meat. Add other ingredients. Cook in 350⁰ F. oven for 1½ hours. Serve with a stuffed baked potatos or stewed rice. Serve hot. Serve 4.

KABOBS WITH ONIONS

2 ears corn on cob, cut in 1½-inch circles
1 lb. beef cut in 1½-inch cubes
2 zucchini squash
4 cherry tomatoes
4 small whole onions
8 large mushrooms

Place all on skewers with alternating colors. Serve on a bed of rice with hand rolls.
SAUCE:
¼ cup diced onions
1 tsp. salt
⅔ cup red wine vinegar
½ tsp. thyme
2 tbsps. oil
½ tsp. dry mustard
1 tbsps. soy sauce
½ tsp. pepper

Marinate sauce: Mix together and place kabobs in sauce and marinate overnight.

BEEF STROGANOFF

1½ lbs. beef tenderloin cut in 1½-inch
   cubes, or beef stew meat
½ tsp. salt
1 lb. mushrooms, sliced
1 can cream of chicken soup
3 medium Vidalia Onions, sliced
2 tbsps. cooking oil
¾ to 1 cup flour
¼ tsp. pepper
1 can water chestnuts, drained
1 can cream of mushroom soup
pint sour cream

Mix flour, salt and pepper together and batter meat. Fry in oil until tender. Add other ingredients, except sour cream. Fold in sour cream last and serve with rice or chow mein noodles. Garnish with whole mushrooms, parsley and carrot curls.

———— • ————

TUNA SALAD

5 cups tuna, flaked
1 cup diced celery
¼ cup Half & Half
⅔ cup mayonnaise
½ tsp. Worcestershire Sauce
1 tbsp. sour cream
Salad greens, use outside greenest
   parts of lettuce
1 medium Vidalia Onion, peeled & chopped
1 cup finely chopped green & red peppers
½ tsp. salt
¼ tsp. red pepper
1 tsp. paprika
Whole or slivered almonds

Mix all ingredients and chill in covered bowl in refrigerator. Arrange on lettuce leaves. Garnish with parsley and tomato wedges and almonds.

GRILLED BAR-B-QUED CHICKEN

3 broiling chickens, 1½-2 lbs. each
cooking oil
½ cup butter, melted
1¾ cups catsup
¾ cup water
⅓ cup vinegar
3 tbsps. brown sugar
1 medium Vidalia Onion, peeled & minced
1½ tbsps. soy sauce
1 tsp. salt
1 tsp. onion salt
1 tsp. dry mustard
½ tsp. prepared mustard
½ tsp. paprika
⅛ tsp. red pepper

Prepare chicken for cooking and place on grill. Wash chickens, split birds in half and remove backbone, neck and keelbone. Bring wing tips back under the shoulder joints. Brush chickens with butter. Arrange chickens on grill and cook 45 minutes or until the drumstick twists off easily. Mix remaining ingredients in a glass saucepan and brush on chickens several times. Chicken should be brown and crisp when done. Heat and serve remaining sauce with chicken.

SAUSAGE/ONION CASSEROLE

1 lb. sausage
1 cup mushrooms, drained
1 can cream of chicken soup
2 cups grated Cheddar cheese
1 can water chestnuts, drained
1 large onion, chopped

Cook sausage over low heat, brown. Add onions and cook 5 minutes longer. Drain grease. Add soup and then all other ingredients and simmer for 10 to 15 minutes, stirring constantly. Do not let cheese go to bottom and burn.

HEARTY MEAT/ONION PIE

First Layer:
1 can biscuits
Second Layer:
½ lb. ground beef
1 medium Vidalia Onion, chopped
½ lb. mushrooms, sliced
1 egg, whole
1 tsp. parsley
½ tsp. salt
¼ tsp. oregano
½ tsp. pepper
Third Layer:
1 cup Swiss cheese, grated
1 cup mild American cheese, grated
3 eggs
¼ cup sour cream
½ cup Half & Half

First Layer: Make a pie shell out of the canned biscuits. Second Layer: Mix next eight ingredients together and cook over low heat. (Do not add egg. Mix egg thoroughly with ingredients so it will help hold pie together.) When done, layer on top of biscuits. Third Layer: Mix next five ingredients together and layer on top of ground beef mixture. Bake in 350⁰ F. oven for 30 to 40 minutes, until brown. Serve hot.

PORK CHOPS WITH ONIONS

4 medium pork chops
3 tbsps. butter
2 tbsps. chives
4 tsps. paprika
1 lb. mushrooms, thick sliced
1 medium Vidalia Onion, sliced

Bake pork chops sprinkled with paprika in 350⁰ F. oven until tender, or about 30 to 40 minutes, covered. Saute' mushrooms, onions, and chives in butter. Pour over pork chops before serving. Garnish with whole mushrooms and sprigs of mint.

STEW

2 lbs. beef stew meat, cut in 1½-inch cubes
¼ tsp. pepper
4 medium Vidalia Onions, sliced
1 rib celery, sliced
2 tbsps. oil
¼ tsp. salt
4 carrots, quartered
6 medium potatoes, quartered

Cook beef stew about 1 hour in salt, pepper and oil until tender. Add vegetables. Cook over low heat until done. Serve with corn bread.

MEAT SAUCE WITH VIDALIA ONIONS

2 tbsps. olive oil
1 lb. lean ground beef
1 lb. mushrooms, thinly sliced, drained
⅛ tsp. red pepper
2 medium Vidalia Onions, chopped
1 28-oz. can tomato paste
½ cup diced red peppers
2 tbsps. chopped parsley
½ cup olives, chopped

Heat oil in saucepan over medium heat. Add onions and meat, cook until tender. Reduce heat to low and add other ingredients. Simmer for 1 to 1½ hours. Tastes delicious over pasta and also as a dip for chips.

SAUSAGE VIDALIA ONION CASSEROLE

1 lb. bulk sausage
1 lb. mushrooms, drained (whole, button, or sliced)
⅛ tsp. red pepper
1 cup slivered almonds
1 box croutons or 3 cups fried bread cubes
2 large Vidalia Onions, chopped
1 can cream of chicken soup
pinch of oregano
pinch of thyme
pinch of marjoram
1 cup cheese

Saute' sausage until done and drain. Add all other ingredients except croutons. Bake in 350⁰ F. oven for 30 minutes. Top with croutons and brown. Serve hot.

———— • ————

CHICKEN & RICE WITH ONIONS

Chicken breasts
2 cups uncooked rice
1 cup milk
4 tbsps. margarine
2 medium onions, sliced
1 can large mushrooms, drained
3 cans cream of chicken soup
1 can cream of mushroom soup
1 can water chestnuts, drained

Place rice in casserole dish and add milk and margarine. Wash chicken breasts and place on top of rice. Mix remaining ingredients together and layer over rice/chicken mixture. Bake at 350⁰ F. for 2 hours. Serve hot. Serves 4.

SALMON CROQUETTES

2 tbsps. margarine
4 tbsps. flour
½ tsp. salt
1 cup salmon or any chopped meat
1 small Vidalia Onion, finely chopped
1 cup milk, evaporated
¼ tsp. pepper
bread crumbs

Saute' onions until translucent. Add flour and gradually add milk and cook until thick. Add salt, pepper and salmon or chopped meat. Cool and add enough bread crumbs to form mixture into a croquette. Dip croquette in crumbs, egg and crumbs again and fry until brown in hot fat. Serve hot. Serves 6.

MEAT LOAF

2 cups ground beef
1 tsp. salt
3 tbsps. flour
½ cup bread crumbs
1 medium Vidalia Onion, chopped
¼ tsp. pepper
1 cup tomato soup, canned
1 cup grated cheese

Mix all ingredients together. Press into a greased loaf pan. Bake in 350° F. oven for an hour. Serves 8.

BEEF ONION LOAF

2 lbs. ground beef
6 slices bacon, chopped fine
1 medium Vidalia Onion, chopped
⅛ tsp. pepper
1 tbsp. chopped parsley
1 egg
¾ cup bread crumbs

Put all ingredients together and make into a loaf. Place in a well greased pan. Preheat oven. Bake at 400° F. for 45 minutes. Serve hot.

BAKED SCALLOPS

1 qt. scallops
2 tbsps. vinegar
Ritz cracker crumbs
3 tbsps. butter
¼ lb. fat, bacon
2 eggs
1 medium Vidalia Onion, chopped

Wash scallops in salt water and drain. Pour boiling water over them. Add the vinegar, let stand for 2 minutes, drain in a colander. Wipe dry. Season fine cracker crumbs. Roll scallops in crumbs, dip in egg, slightly beaten and add crumbs. Saute' onions in butter, lay scallops close together in a shallow pan and top with onions. Cut the sliced bacon in narrow strips and scatter over the scallops. Bake in 350° oven for 25 to 35 minutes. Serves 6. Can top with grated cheese and garnish with parsley.

SHRIMP AU GRATIN

3 tbsps. butter
1 medium Vidalia Onion, chopped
1 large can crab meat
2 cans shrimp
4 tbsps. butter
1 tsp. salt
¼ tsp. black pepper
1½ cups milk
½ cup grated cheese
3 tbsps. flour

Saute' onions in butter, and make white sauce with flour, milk, salt, pepper, butter and cheese. Cook until done. Cover bottom of casserole dish with thin white sauce. Add layer of crab meat and shrimp alternating layers until dish is filled. Cover with cheese. Dot with fat. Bake at 500° F. for 12 minutes or until bubbly. Serves 6.

LOBSTER & ONION CASSEROLE

2 medium Vidalia Onions, chopped
1 lb. mushrooms
5½ tbsps. butter
3 tbsps. flour
1 tsp. salt
⅛ tsp. paprika
1½ cups milk
½ cup bouillon stock
½ cup Half & Half
2 cups canned or fresh lobster meat
⅓ cup bread crumbs
3 egg yolks

Wash, peel and chop onions. Slice mushrooms. Saute' them in fat, and add flour, salt, and paprika. Cool 5 minutes. Then gradually add milk and bouillon stock. Cook 3 minutes. Add lobster meat, cut in pieces, and the Half & Half. Beat egg yolks well and add to mixture. Pour into a greased casserole dish. Cover the top with the dried bread crumbs. Add 1½ tbsps. of fat in bits. Bake at 350⁰ F. for 20 minutes. Serves 6.

GROUND BEEF DISH

1 lb. ground beef, cooked & drained
2 cups potatoes, diced
½ cup Ritz cracker crumbs
½ cup grated cheese
1 medium Vidalia Onion, chopped
1 egg
½ cups evaporated milk
2 tbsps. butter
Parsley

Cook ground beef and onions, drain and add potatoes and milk and pour into a greased baking dish. Spread with the egg beaten lightly. Cover with crumbs, mixed with fat and sprinkle with cheese. Bake at 500⁰ F. for 15 minutes. Garnish with parsley. Serves 6.

SAUSAGE WITH ONIONS

1 lb. sausage, seasoned
½ bell pepper, chopped
1 can French Fried Onion Rings
2 medium Vidalia Onions, chopped
1 can cream of chicken soup

Brown sausage and add onions and peppers. Add soup. Cook in oven at 350⁰ F. for 1 hour. Top with French Fried Onion Rings and brown. Serves 6.

——————— • ———————

CHINESE CHICKEN WITH VIDALIA ONIONS

4 whole chicken breasts
1 tbsp. dry white wine
3 medium Vidalia Onions, chopped
7 tbsps. Safflower oil
⅛ tsp. garlic
2 tbsps. cornstarch
4 tbsps. soy sauce
⅛ tsp. salt
3 red or green peppers, chopped
1¼ cup raw cashews (not dry roasted)
2 tsps. sugar

Skin, bone and cut chicken into bite size pieces. Marinate for 2 hours in refrigerator in soy sauce, wine, cornstarch, sugar and garlic. Boil raw nuts in water 10 to 15 minutes. If regular cashews, boil 1 to 2 minutes. Drain. Heat 2 tbsps. oil in wok and cook cashews 10 minutes. Wipe pan and add 3 tbsps. oil, add chicken and marinate. Fry 5 minutes. Remove. Use 1 tbsp. oil in wok and cook green pepper and onion 3 minutes. Add chicken and cashews. Serve all hot on a platter. Serve with rice if desired.

CHICKEN SUPREME

6 chicken breasts
½ clove garlic
6 sprigs parsley
1 can condensed tomato soup
flour
6 tbsps. margarine
6 medium size Vidalia Onions,
  chopped fine
1 sprig mint
2 tsps. salt
pepper

Place margarine in a frying pan with clove of garlic, onions, parsley and mint. Flour chicken, add salt and pepper. Cook chicken until lightly browned, then add condensed tomato soup and mix well. Thicken the gravy, allowing 1 tbsp. of flour to each cup of broth. Pour the gravy over the chicken and serve with rice and currant jelly. Serves 6.

———— • ————

ROAST BEEF WITH ONIONS

1 4-lb. beef eye or round roast
1 lb. fresh mushrooms, sliced
1 can water chestnuts, drained
½ cup dry bread cubes
4 medium Vidalia Onions, sliced
4 tbsps. butter
1 bay leaf
2 cups grated mild American cheese

Place roast in large casserole dish. Combine other ingredients except bread crumbs and place on top of roast. Cook at 350° F. for 30 minutes to 1 hour, according to doneness desired in roast. Remove and top with bread cubes and return to oven until brown.

HAM / ONION FILLING

4 tbsps. butter
4 tbsps. flour
1½ cups milk, evaporated
1 tsp. salt
½ tsp. freshly ground pepper
¼ cup sour cream
1 tbsp. parsley
2 medium onions, chopped, cooked
1 lb. mushrooms, sliced, cooked
2 cups cooked ham, diced
12 plain crepes
⅔ cup grated Cheddar cheese

Blend butter and flour over heat. Stir in milk and simmer until thickened. Add seasonings, stirring constantly. Fold in sour cream and remaining ingredients. DO NOT BOIL AT ANYTIME. Spread crepes with filling and roll. Place in a shallow baking dish. Sprinkle with cheese and put under broiler to glaze. Serves 6. Garnish with a fresh mushroom or strawberry preserves.

SWEET AND SOUR PORK CHOPS

4 ½- to ¾-inch thick pork chops
Salt and pepper to taste
2 tbsps. salad oil
1 lemon, sliced
2 Vidalia Onions, sliced thick
¾ cup catsup
½ cup water
2 tbsps. firmly packed brown sugar

Season chops with salt and pepper; brown in hot oil; drain well. Place chops in a shallow dish; top with lemon slices. Combine catsup, water and sugar; blend well. Pour sauce over chops; top with thick slice of Vidalia Onion. Cover with foil and bake at 350° F. for one hour.

Marianne McMillan

RABBIT IN AN ONION SAUCE

1 rabbit
1 tsp. salt
½ tsp. sage
6 tbsps. margarine
3 strips bacon
⅓ cup flour
½ tsp. coarse black pepper
¼ tsp. paprika
1 medium Vidalia Onion, chopped
4 cups thin white sauce

Dress and clean 1 rabbit and disjoint in pieces of serving. Mix flour, salt, pepper, sage and paprika into a bowl. Thoroughly coat the rabbit with this mixture. Saute' in the 3 tbsps. margarine in a casserole and lay the bacon over the surface. Saute' onions in 3 tbsps. margarine until translucent. Make the white sauce and add saute'ed onions to sauce. Pour over and around the rabbit. Bake in 375⁰ F. preheated oven for 2 hours or until done. Serves 6 to 8. Can serve on a bed of rice and garnish with parsley or boiled egg slices around platter of cooked rabbit.

MEATBALLS

20-25 Ritz crackers
1 medium Vidalia Onion, diced
½ lb. ground cooked pork
1 tsp. salt
½ tsp. pepper, coarse, black
1½ cups milk
1 tbsp. butter
½ lb. ground beef
2 eggs
1 tsp. soy sauce
Extra butter to saute' meatballs

Crumble crackers into milk. Let stand 6 minutes. Saute' onion in butter until translucent. Combine all ingredients and mix well. Shape into 25 small balls. Saute' in frying pan in butter until brown and thoroughly cooked.

CREAMED CHICKEN

3 tbsps. butter
3 tbsps. flour
¼ tsp. dry mustard
½ tsp. paprika
1 cup evaporated milk
1 tsp. lemon juice
2 hard-cooked eggs, cut coarsely
4 slices toast or crackers
1 medium Vidalia Onion, diced
½ tsp. salt
¼ tsp. prepared mustard
¼ tsp. pepper, red
1 3-oz. can mushrooms, sliced
½ tsp. soy sauce
1 6½ oz. can deboned chicken

Saute' onions in butter and stir in flour and seasonings. Stir in milk gradually. Cook, stirring until slightly thickened. Add mushrooms and then liquid. Stir in lemon juice and soy sauce. Add eggs and chicken meat. Mix and let heat thoroughly. Serve on toast or crackers. Makes 4 servings.

BEEF STROGANOFF

2 lbs. beef stew, cut in
  bite size pieces
2 medium onions, chopped
1 tsp. salt
½ tsp. pepper
1 lb. mushrooms, sliced
1 can water chestnuts, drained
1 can cream of chicken soup
1 can cream of mushroom soup
8 oz. sour cream

Brown meat; add onions, salt and pepper, mushrooms and water chestnuts. Add soups. Take off heat and add sour cream. Serve on a bed of chow mein noodles or rice. Serves 8.

BROILED SALMON WITH ONIONS

2 salmon steaks, 1½-inch thick
1 tsp. salt
½ tsp. freshly ground pepper
1 tbsp. olive oil or as desired
1 cup Hollandaise Sauce
1 8-oz. pkg. cream cheese
2 medium onions, sliced
4 tbsps. butter
½ tsp. paprika
2 tbsps. caviar

Season steaks with salt and pepper, brush with olive oil and broil until done. Blend onions and cream cheese until smooth, add paprika. Spread this mixture over the steaks. Add caviar to the Hollandaise Sauce and serve with salmon. Serves 4.

DELICIOUS ROASTED CHICKEN

4 lbs. roasting chicken
2 tbsps. olive oil
1 tsp. salt
¼ cup Vidalia Onions, diced
¼ cup green peppers, diced
¼ cup red peppers, diced
⅓ cup water chestnuts, sliced
⅓ cup mushrooms, sliced
¼ cup cubed baked ham
4 ripe tomatoes, peeled & quartered
1 tsp. salt
½ tsp. fresh ground pepper

Roast chicken in 350⁰ F. oven for 1½ hours or until done. Heat olive oil and saute' onions, peppers, mushrooms, water chestnuts and baked ham. Add tomatoes, salt and pepper. Cover and cook gently until tomatoes are soft. Cut the chicken into quarters and cover with the sauce. Serve very hot on rice. Garnish with a fresh mushroom, parsley, pimento, or egg slices. Serves 6.

————— • —————

CRAB / ONION CASSEROLE

2 cans crab, drained
2 tbsps. margarine
2 medium onions, chopped
2 cups Cheddar cheese
½ cup olives, minced
1 can cream of chicken soup
2 cups croutons

Saute' onions in margarine. Take from heat and add all other ingredients. Cook at 350⁰ F. for ½ hour. Remove and top with croutons, brown. Serve hot. Serves 4.

CRANBERRY STUFFED LAMB CHOPS

4 lamb shoulder chops, ¾-inch thick
cooking oil
1½ cups whole cranberries, chopped
¼ cup sugar
¼ cup chopped celery
¼ cup chopped Vidalia Onions
¼ cup butter or margarine
½-8-oz. pkg. herb seasoned stuffing mix
1 medium orange, sectioned and chopped
½ cup chopped pecans

In skillet brown chops in oil 10 to 15 minutes. Remove from pan; drain fat. Combine cranberries and sugar; let stand a few minutes. Cook celery and onion in butter until tender. Remove from heat; stir in stuffing mix and 1 cup water. Mix well. Stir in cranberries, oranges and pecans. Then into baking dish, 13 x 9 x 2-inch. Top with chops. Sprinkle with salt and pepper. Cover; bake in 350⁰ F. oven for 45 minutes. Uncover; bake 10 minutes. Serves 4.

"O-DEER"

1½ lbs. ground venison
2 jumbo Vidalia Onions
2 small chopped green Vidalia Onions
¼ lb. Mozzarella cheese, grated
2 medium banana peppers, chopped
½ tsp. salt
½ tsp. pepper
½ tsp. chili powder
2 tbsps. Worcestershire Sauce
12 strips of red rind hoop cheese
   ½-inch wide, ⅛-inch thick &
   3-inches long

Boil jumbo onions until soft enough to separate into sections. Combine remaining ingredients (except hoop cheese). Stuff onion shells with mixture. Bake at 350⁰ F. for 30 minutes. Top each stuffed onion shell with 2 slices of hoop cheese and place in oven until cheese melts. Remove and serve.

James "Red" Castleman

Vegetables, Casseroles

The generous use of many vegetables, served either alone or in a casserole, contribute to sound health and vitality.

Most dark green and deep yellow vegetables excell as dependable and inexpensive sources of Vitamin A and Vitamin C. Some of these vegetables are good sources of potassium, folic acid, Vitamin B[6] and fiber.

Fresh vegetables and vegetables prepared without seasonings are excellent for people on diets. Cooked and raw vegetables have very few calories.

BLUE DEVIL ONIONS

4 medium Vidalia Onions, thinly
   sliced & separated into rings
1 3-oz. pkg. blue cheese,
   crumbled (about ¾ cup)
½ cup salad oil
2 tbsps. lemon juice
1 tsp. salt
½ tsp. sugar
dash of pepper
dash of paprika

Place onion rings in shallow dish. Combine remaining ingredients thoroughly; pour over onions and stir to coat onions well. Refrigerate at least 3 to 4 hours. Makes about 1 qt.

ONIONS GOURMET

6 medium Vidalia Onions, sliced &
   separated into rings
½ tsp. monosodium glutamate
½ tsp. salt
¼ cup butter
½ cup cooking sherry
¼ cup parmesan cheese
½ tsp. fresh ground pepper

Season onions with monosodium glutamate, salt, and pepper. Cook in butter till tender, but not brown, about 8 minutes, tossing to stir. Add sherry; cook rapidly 2-3 minutes. Sprinkle with Parmesan cheese. Serve in sauce dishes. Serves 8.

GOLDEN ONION RINGS

Cut 6 medium Bermuda or mild white onions into slices ¼-thick; separate into rings. Combine 1 cup plus 2 tbsps. sifted all-purpose flour, ½ tsp. salt, 1 slightly beaten egg, 1 cup milk, and 2 tbsps. salad oil. Beat together just till dry ingredients are well moistened. Coat onion rings with batter. Fry, a few at a time, in deep hot fat (375⁰ F.), stirring once to separate rings. When onions are golden, drain on paper towels. Just before serving, sprinkle with salt.

———— • ————

ONION-MUSHROOM CASSEROLE

2 lbs. (4 cups) small
   Vidalia Onions
¼ cup butter
1 can canned mushrooms, stems &
   pieces or 1½ cups sliced fresh
   mushrooms
3 tbsps. flour
1½ cups milk
¼ cup shredded Cheddar cheese
¼ cup cracker crumbs
1 3-oz. pkg. cream cheese

Combine onions with butter, mushrooms and salt; simmer 5 minutes. Add cream cheese. When melted, add flour, then milk and reheat. Turn into 1½ or 2 qt. casserole. Sprinkle with mixture of shredded cheese and crumbs. Bake in hot oven (400⁰ F.) for 25 to 30 minutes. Makes 5 servings.

ONION CUSTARD

2 slices bacon
3 cups sliced and quartered
   Vidalia Onions
1 cup water
1 13-oz. can evaporated milk
⅓ cup water
1 tsp. salt
⅛ tsp. pepper
1 tsp. crushed dill weed or
   dill seeds

Fry bacon; remove from skillet and crumble. Pour bacon fat from skillet. Add onions and 1 cup water; cook 10 minutes; drain. In mixing bowl, combine remaining ingredients; stir in bacon and onions. Pour into 1½ qt. casserole. Set in pan of water. Bake in moderate oven 375⁰ F. for 35 to 40 minutes, or until knife inserted halfway between edge and center comes out clean. Makes 6 servings.

———— • ————

ONION AND POTATO CASSEROLE

6 large Vidalia Onions, sliced
6 large white potatoes
2 cans condensed mushroom soup
4 tbsps. fat
2 tbsps. salt on meat
2 lbs. lean ground beef

Season meat and brown in hot fat. Peel and slice potatoes, thinly. Make alternate layers of potatoes, onions and meat. Pour mushroom soup on top and bake at 350⁰ F. for 45 minutes.

STUFFED VIDALIA ONIONS

1 large Vidalia sweet Onion (approx.
  1 cup) sliced crosswise
1 tbsp. butter, melted
⅛ tsp. salt
1 cup dry herb bread stuffing
¼ cup beef broth
¼ tsp. pepper

In 1½ qt. casserole place piece of plastic wrap large enough to wrap stuffed onion. In a 4 cup measuring cup mix dry stuffing, beef broth, melted butter, salt & pepper. Mixture should be moist but not soggy.

Place bottom slice of onion on plastic wrap. Top with a little less than ½ stuffing mixture. Add middle slice of onion, top with rest of stuffing mixture, leaving approximately 1 tbsp. in measuring cup. Take top onion slice and cut a hole in center just large enough for remaining stuffing mixture. Place this sliced of onion on top of stack, fill center with remaining stuffing.

Pull up edges of plastic wrap and tie loosely with string. Cook on high 6 minutes. Let stand approximately 10 minutes. When done, onion should be tender when pierced with a fork. Serves 2.

Note: Larger onions will require longer cooking.

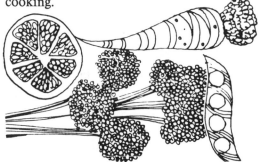

SAUTEÉD ONIONS

4 onions, sliced ¼-inch thick
3 tbsps. butter or margarine

Preheat Multi-Cooker Frypan to 300ºF. Add butter and melt. Add onions and saute', stirring frequently until golden in color. Sprinkle with salt. Serve over chops, hamburgers, steak or liver, etc. 4 servings.

——————— • ———————

ACORN SQUASH WITH CREAMED ONIONS

3 acorn squash (salted to taste)
2 lbs. small Vidalia Onions
  peeled (about 4 cups)
½ cup light raisins
¼ tsp. salt
1½ cups milk
¼ tsp. ground nutmeg
2 tbsps. flour

Wash squash; cut in halves lengthwise and remove seeds. Place squash, cut side down, in shallow baking dish; add a few tbsps. water to dish. Bake in hot oven (400º F) 30 minutes. Turn cut side up; sprinkle with salt and continue baking 25 to 30 minutes, until tender. Cook onions in boiling salted water, covered, about 30 minutes or till tender. Drain. Simmer raisins in water to cover 10 minutes, drain. Melt butter; blend in flour and ¼ tsp. salt. Add milk all at once. Cook and stir until sauce is thickened. Blend in ¼ tsp. nutmeg. Gently stir in onions and raisins. Spoon into cooked squash halves; sprinkle with additional nutmeg. Creamed onions deluxe fill baked squash cups for an extra good dish.

ONIONS A LA CREQUE

36-40 Small Vidalia Onions
4 tbsps. olive oil
⅔ cup white wine
½ cup water
1 tsp. sugar
1 cup currants or sultana raisins
1 tsp. salt
Sprig of fennel
½ tsp. thyme
1 bay leaf
Pinch of saffron

Peel onions and place in a skillet. Add oil, wine, water, sugar and seasonings except saffron and currants or raisins and cook down. Remove onions and reduce the sauce. Pour sauce over onions. Serve cool. Serves 6-8. Variation - 1 or 2 tbsps. tomato paste.

———— • ————

ONIONS AU GRATIN

2½ cups cooked Vidalia Onions
2½ cups grated Cheddar cheese
¼ cup self-rising flour
3 tbsps. butter or oleo
Salt to taste
Pepper to taste

Cut onions into quarters before cooking. Cook in boiling water till tender. Drain and mix with other ingredients, reserving ½ cup of the grated cheese. Pour into casserole dish and cover with reserved cheese. Bake at 350⁰F for 20 to 30 minutes.

SWEET ONION CONFETTI

Combine 2 cups chopped onions, ½ bell pepper, 3 tbsps. diced pimento; set aside. Combine ¼ cup vinegar, ¼ cup water, ¼ cup sugar, 2 tsps. caraway seeds, ½ tsp. salt and simmer for 5 minutes. Pour over onions, refrigerate for several hours.

———— • ————

ONIONS AU GRATIN

Boil onions until done, cut each onion into quarters. Put into baking dish - - onion, white sauce, grated cheese, cracker crumbs; repeat until dish is full. Cover top with buttered cracker crumbs and put in oven to just heat through and brown top.

———— • ————

ONION SOUP

Cook 1 cup chopped Vidalia Sweet Onion (1 large) in 3 tbsps. butter till tender but not brown. Blend in 3 tbsps. all-purpose flour, ½ tsp. salt, and dash of pepper. Add 4 cups milk all at once. Heat and stir till boiling. Remove from heat. Add 2 cups shredded sharp process American Cheese, stirring to melt cheese. Serves 4 to 6.

———— • ————

SWEET AND SOUR ONIONS

4 large Vidalia Onions
¼ cup cider vinegar
½ cup melted butter
½ cup boiling water
½ cup brown sugar

Slice onions and arrange in 1 qt. baking dish. Mix rest of ingredients and pour over onions. Bake at 300⁰ F for 1 hour.

STUFFED ONIONS

6 large Vidalia Sweet Onions
1 cup ripe olives
½ cup shredded Cheddar cheese
2 tbsps. minced parsley
¼ tsp. poultry seasoning
Dash pepper
½ cup butter or margarine
1 cup soft bread crumbs
Paprika
½ tsp. salt
¼ tsp. sage

Peel onions, removing thin outer layer only. Slice off tops of onions, making them as even in height as possible. Cover with boiling, salted water and simmer for 30 minutes, or until just tender. Drain and cool. Chop onion tops to make ⅓ cup finely chopped onion; saute' in butter until golden brown. Chop olives and combine with bread crumbs, cheese, parsley, salt, pepper, poultry seasoning and sage. Scoop out center portion of onions (set aside, chop, and add to creamed peas for another meal, if desired). Do not cut through bottom of onion "shells". Fill with olive mixture; sprinkle with paprika. Bake, covered, in moderate oven for 20 minutes. Uncover and bake 10 minutes longer. Serve piping hot.

————— • —————

WEST COAST ONIONS

Place 2 cups thinly sliced Vidalia Onions in a shallow dish. Pour over them ½ cup water and enough vinegar to cover. Sprinkle with 1 tsp. sugar. Cover dish and let chill 3 to 4 hours. Just before serving, drain onions and mix with ¼ tsp. celery seed and salt to taste.

CRUNCHY GLAZED ONIONS

Use 1½ lbs. small, white peeled Vidalia Sweet Onions, 3 tbsps. butter or margarine, 2 tbsps. brown sugar, ⅓ cup roasted diced almonds. Cook onions in boiling water until fork tender, about 25 minutes, then drain well. In saucepan, combine butter, brown sugar and almonds. Cook, stirring occasionally, until butter and sugar are melted. Add onions and heat thoroughly, turning onions to coat with glaze. Serves 5 to 6.

————— • —————

CREAMED PEAS
IN ONION CUPS

12 medium Vidalia Onions
6 cups boiling water
2 tsps. salt
3 tbsps. butter
2 tbsps. flour
few grains pepper
1 cup milk
1½ cups cooked or canned peas

Peel onions and cook, uncovered in boiling water to which 1½ tsps. salt have been added, 30 minutes or until almost tender. Drain. Scoop out center with sharp paring knife to form cups. Put in baking dish with 2 tbsps. butter melted. Bake in hot oven (400⁰ F.) for 30 minutes, or until lightly browned, basting frequently with melted butter. Meanwhile, melt remaining tbsp. butter in saucepan. Blend in flour, remaining ½ tsp. salt and pepper. Stir in milk slowly. Boil 2 minutes, stirring constantly. Add peas and heat thoroughly. To serve, fill onion cups with creamed peas. Serves 6.

VIDALIA ONION CASSEROLE WITH ALMONDS

2 tbsps. butter
2 tbsps. flour
1 cup chicken broth
½ cup light cream
3 cups wedged Vidalia Onions, parboiled
½ cup sliced almonds
½ tsp. salt
½ tsp. pepper
1 cup fine bread crumbs
½ cup grated Cheddar cheese

Melt butter; stir in flour. Add broth and cream, stirring constantly until thick and smooth. Add onions, almonds and seasonings; pour into buttered 1½ qt. casserole. Cover with crumbs and cheese. Place in pan of water. Bake at 375° F. for 35 minutes. Yield: 6 servings.

ONIONS A LA CREOLE

6 to 8 Vidalia Onions
2 tbsps. chopped green pepper
Salt and pepper
½ cup chopped celery
1 to 1½ cups tomato juice
2 tbsps. butter

Arrange onions in casserole; add remaining ingredients and bake covered at 350° degrees for about 1 hour. Yield: 6 servings.

LYONNAISE POTATOES

4 cups boiled potatoes
6 tbsps. butter
2 medium Vidalia Onions, chopped
2 cups cheese

Cook onions in 2 tbsps. butter. Then add potatoes and add rest of fat. Let cook until fat is taken up; add cheese. Season with salt, pepper, and paprika.

LIMA BEANS WITH ONIONS

2 cups lima beans
3 medium sized onions
1 tsp. salt
1 cup bread crumbs
½ lb. sliced bacon
1 cup milk
½ tsp. pepper
1 tbsp. butter

Brown bacon and remove from frying pan. Cook the chopped onions in the fat until tender. Then combine all the ingredients, place in a greased casserole, and bake in a slow oven until the beans are tender, adding more milk if needed.

————— • —————

BAKED CABBAGE WITH ONIONS

2 cups boiled cabbage
1 tbsp. flour
¾ cup bread crumbs
½ tsp. salt
dash paprika
2 medium onions, sliced
6 tbsps. butter
1 cup milk
dash pepper
1 cup cheese

Spray pan with PAM or grease. Saute' onions in 4 tbsps. butter. Place a thin layer of cabbage in a baking dish, sprinkle with a little of the flour, salt and pepper; dot with some butter and cover with a layer of bread crumbs. Repeat having bread crumbs on top. Pour on the milk and sprinkle with cheese. Bake 20 to 30 minutes in a slow oven until the top is browned nicely.

TURNIP GREENS WITH ONIONS

1 bunch turnip greens
2 medium Vidalia Onions, chopped or
  sliced
4 pieces bacon

Fry bacon in bottom of pan, add onions and then add water and turnip greens. Cook for 30 minutes until tender. Cook with a small amount of water and in a covered container.

CORN AND ONIONS

1¾ cup corn
¾ lb. bacon
½ tsp. salt
1 medium Vidalia Onion, chopped
dash pepper

Cut the sliced bacon in squares and brown in a frying pan with the onions. When delicately browned, pour off some of the fat, leaving 5 to 6 tbsps. in the pan. Add the corn, salt and pepper. Cook 5 minutes. Serve hot.

EGGPLANT ONION CASSEROLE

1 eggplant, washed and cleaned
2 tbsps. butter
½ cup Swiss cheese, grated
1 cup mild American cheese, grated
1 large can tomato paste
2 medium Vidalia Onions, sliced
1 cup sour cream
½ cup Monterey Jack cheese, grated
1 cup Caraway Seed cheese, grated
1 cup catsup

Spray casserole dish with PAM. Fry eggplant and line bottom of casserole dish. Saute' onions in butter and layer. Mix other ingredients together and layer. Cook at 350⁰ F. for 30 to 45 minutes. Serve hot.

CREAMED SPINACH WITH ONIONS

1½ cups spinach
1 tbsp. flour
½ tsp. salt
dash paprika
1½ cups milk
4 tbsps. butter
dash pepper
1 medium Vidalia Onion, chopped

Saute' onions in 3 tbsps. butter. Thicken the milk with the flour and add salt, pepper and butter. Stir in spinach and other ingredients. Top with grated cheese if desired and cook in 350⁰ F. oven 20 to 30 minutes. Serve on slices of toast or biscuits.

ONIONS BAKED ON COALS

Wrap large peeled Vidalia Onions in aluminum foil as you do for baked potatoes. Place them in hot ashes until steak and potatoes are ready. Remove from the ashes and ENJOY.

GREEN BEANS/ONION CASSEROLE

1 can green beans, drained
1 can water chestnuts, sliced and drained
1 cup cracker crumbs, saltine
1 can French Fried Onion Rings
1 lb. mushrooms, sliced and drained
1 medium Vidalia Onion, chopped
1 egg
2 cups grated cheese

Mix all ingredients except onion rings together and bake at 350⁰ F. for 30 minutes. Top with French Fried Onion Rings.

BAKED BEANS WITH ONIONS

1 medium can pork and beans
1 medium bell pepper, chopped
1 tbsp. brown sugar
1 medium Vidalia Onion, chopped
2 cups grated mild American Cheese

Mix all ingredients together and bake at 350° F for 20 to 30 minutes. Serve hot. Can top with grated cheese if desired.

SQUASH CASSEROLE WITH ONIONS
$1,000 RECIPE

3 cups canned or frozen squash, cooked and drained
2 eggs
1 tbsp. margarine
2 cups Ritz crackers, crushed
1 medium Vidalia Onion, finely chopped
2 cups cheese, grated, mild American
1 tbsp. milk
1 small can cream of chicken soup

1. Cook squash according to package directions. DRAIN. 2. Mix all other ingredients together with squash. 3. Grease baking pan with PAM. 4. Cook casserole about 30 to 40 minutes, or until browned on top 350° F. oven. Seabrook Farm/McKenzie.

STIR FRY VEGETABLES

2 lbs. fresh broccoli
1 lb. fresh mushrooms
3 tbsps. oil
2 medium onions, sliced
1 can water chestnuts, drained and sliced
2 tsps. soy sauce

Put oil in wok and add vegetables and soy sauce. Cook for 5 to 7 minutes. Serve hot.

FRIED POTATO/ ONION CASSEROLE

4 large potatoes, sliced
3 cups grated mild American cheese
3 large Vidalia Onions, sliced

In a skillet slice potatoes and onions and fry with 3 tbsps. margarine. After done, add 3 cups grated cheese and simmer for 10 to 15 minutes, serve immediately.

CREAMED ONIONS

1½ cups onions, chopped
4 tbsps. flour
1 cup rich milk
⅛ tsp. pepper
½ cup mushrooms, sliced and drained
3 tbsps. butter or chicken fat
1 cup stock
½ tsp. paprika
½ tsp. salt

Melt butter and saute' onions until translucent. Add flour and stir over low heat until blended. Add cold stock and milk at once. Stir and cook over low heat until thickened and smooth. Set over hot water; add mushrooms, heat thoroughly. Serve hot in timbales or toast, or shortcake fashion on squares of hot cornbread.

ONION GRITS CASSEROLE

2 medium Vidalia Onions, grated
1 tsp. salt
2½ cups boiling water
2 tbsps. butter
1 cup grits
2 cups grated cheese

Saute' onions in margarine. Have grits ready, preparing as instructed on package directions. Add cheese and onions to grits.

ONION, CHEESE, RICE CASSEROLE

1 stick margarine
1¾ cups uncooked rice
1½ cups blanched, slivered almonds
1 lb. grated Cheddar cheese
1 large Vidalia Onion, chopped
2 cans beef consomme or bouillon
1 lb. fresh mushrooms, sliced

Saute' onions in butter. Mix all ingredients together and place in a casserole dish. Bake uncovered 15 minutes at 300⁰ F. Stir occasionally.

ONION EGG CASSEROLE

2 cups croutons or fried bread cubes
5 eggs
¼ tsp. salt
dash red pepper
1½ cups cheese, grated
1 cup milk
½ tsp. mustard, prepared
8 sliced bacon, cooked & crumbled

Grease casserole dish. Line bottom of dish with croutons and layer with grated cheese. Combine all other ingredients (save bacon) together and mix. Pour over croutons and cheese and sprinkle cooked bacon on top. Can also use ham if desired. Bake uncovered 35 to 40 minutes in 350⁰ F. oven.

BAKED BEANS WITH ONIONS

1 medium can pork & beans
1 medium bell pepper, chopped
1 tsp. mustard
2 medium onions, chopped
3 tbsps. catsup
¼ cup brown sugar

Mix all ingredients together and bake at 325⁰ F. for 40 minutes. Serve hot.

GREEN BEANS WITH VIDALIA ONIONS

1 can green beans, drained
1 can cream of chicken soup
1 can water chestnuts, drained & sliced
2 cups croutons or fried bread cubes
3 medium Vidalia Onions, sliced
½ tsp. soy sauce
½ tsp. red pepper
1 or 2 tbsps. margarine or butter

Arrange green beans in casserole dish. Add onions. Mix other ingredients together and pour on top of vegetables. Cook at 350⁰ F. for 30 minutes. Top with croutons. Can dot with margarine or butter. Return to oven until brown.

GRILLED ONIONS

Peel onions, sprinkle on salt and pepper, add a large amount of butter, wrap in foil and bake at 350⁰ F. until tender.

GREEN BEAN CASSEROLE WITH VIDALIA ONIONS

1 can green beans, drained
1 cup wheat thins, crushed
1 can water chestnuts, drained & sliced
1 can French Fried Onion Rings
1¼ cups Cheddar cheese, grated
2 eggs, whole
1 can cream of chicken soup
1 lb. mushrooms, sliced
   drained if canned
1 medium Vidalia Onion, chopped

Mix all together except for the French Fried Onion Rings. Bake at 350⁰ F. for 30 minutes. Take out of oven and add 1 can of French Fried Onion Rings. Brown. Serve hot.

CRUNCHY ASPARAGUS WITH VIDALIA ONIONS

Fresh asparagus spears
½ tsp. salt
½ tsp. coarse black pepper
4 tbsps. oil
3 medium Vidalia Onions, sliced
⅛ tsp. oregano

Slice asparagus diagonally. Place oil in wok and heat. Add asparagus, onion, and other seasonings. Cover and shake until crispy, about 6 to 8 minutes.

MUSHROOM / POTATO & ONION SUPREME

3 tbsps. butter
1 lb. fresh mushrooms, thick sliced
1 can cream of chicken soup
4 medium potatoes, quartered
2 medium Vidalia Onions, sliced

Saute' potatoes, mushrooms, and onions in butter until done, leave crispy! Add cream of chicken soup. Cook until hot and serve. Do not over cook!! Garnish with parsley sprigs.

VEGETABLES TO GARNISH ROAST

Place roast in center of platter and garnish with these vegetables:

3 tbsps. butter
1 lb. mushrooms, sliced
1 carrot, sliced thin
3 medium onions, sliced
1 can water chestnuts, sliced, drained

Mix all ingredients and saute' in butter. Arrange around roast. Serve with biscuits or popovers. Garnish with parsley sprigs.

MARINATED CARROTS AND ONIONS

12 carrots, cleaned, sliced, peeled
1 bottle Catalina Dressing
4 medium onions, sliced

Mix together and serve with crackers. Needs to marinate overnight.

SWEET CORN

6 ears corn
1½ cups milk
⅛ tsp. black pepper
3 tbsps. butter
½ tsp. salt
1 medium onion, chopped

Cut the kernels from cobs and place in a frying pan with butter, and add onions. Cook 12 minutes. Add milk, salt, and pepper. As soon as milk is hot, the corn is ready to be served.

STUFFED BAKED POTATOES

4 medium baking potatoes
4 oz. cream cheese
dash pepper
1 cup grated cheese
¼ cup butter or margarine
½ tsp. salt
1 large onion, diced

Wash, scrub, and bake potatoes at 350⁰ F. for 45 minutes to 1 hour until done. Take insides out of potatoes and mix with the remaining ingredients. Top with extra cheese, crumbled bacon, or ham. • If cheese, return to oven to melt. • Please use 5 to 6 potatoes if planning for a party because they often tear up.

VIDALIA ONION PIE

1 pie crust, make holes with fork,
  uncooked
1 tsp. salt
½ lb. Ricotta cheese
1 cup grated mild American cheese
⅛ tsp. nutmeg
2 tbsps. butter
2 medium Vidalia Onions, sliced
⅛ tsp. pepper
3 eggs, beaten
¼ cup Half & Half
¼ cup sour cream

Bake pie shell 10 minutes. Saute onions in butter. Mix all other ingredients together and pour over onions. Bake at 350⁰ F. for 30 to 40 minutes. Serve with a salad and fruit dessert.

———— • ————

PAPRIKA ONIONS

1 can cream of mushroom soup
4 large sweet onions, peeled & cut
  4 times in top center, only
  ¼ way down and squeeze
1 tsp. Worcestershire Sauce
½ cup water
5 tbsps. butter or margarine
paprika
½ tsp. salt
1 cup Cheddar cheese, grated

Preheat oven to 350⁰ F. Pour soup in bottom of casserole dish. Arrange onions in greased casserole dish. (Grease & butter). Mix all ingredients together and put in top of onions. Bake 1½ hours or until onions are tender. Sprinkle with additional paprika and cheese if desired. Makes 4 to 8 servings.

ESCALLOPED ONIONS AND CHEESE

2 large onions, peeled & boiled
¼ cup sifted all-purpose flour
½ tsp. paprika
¼ tsp. celery salt
1 cup mild American cheese, grated
4 tbsps. butter or margarine
2 cups milk, evaporated
1 tsp. salt
1 tsp. mustard, dry
1 can French Fried Onion Rings

Preheat oven to 350⁰ F. Melt butter in saucepan. Add flour until smooth. Slowly add milk, stirring constantly. Add seasonings. Add cheese and cook until creamy and smooth. Remember to keep stirring. Place onions in a casserole dish and add sauce over onions. Bake 20 minutes until hot and bubbly. Top with French Fried Onion Rings and return to oven to brown.

VEGETABLE MEDLEY

4 cucumbers, peeled and cubed
¾ cup mayonnaise
⅛ tsp. pepper
2 medium Vidalia Onions, chopped
2 tbsps. chopped parsley
1 bell pepper, diced
10 radishes, sliced
½ tsp. salt
¼ to ½ cup cottage cheese
1 rib celery, diced
¼ of a whole cauliflower, washed
  & flowered

Mix all together, cleaning all vegetables and chopping them. Serve as a salad. Can add more mayonnaise or cottage cheese as desired.

ONION CASSEROLE

6 medium Vidalia Onions, sliced
1 pt. sour cream
1 can water chestnuts, drained
½ tsp. paprika
¼ cup mayonnaise
¼ cup butter
1 can cream of chicken soup
2 cups Cheddar cheese, grated
2 cups crushed Ritz crackers

In greased casserole dish, arrange onion. Mix together other ingredients and pour over onions. Bake at 350⁰ F. for 30 to 40 minutes. Top with cracker crumbs. Dot with mayonnaise. Serve hot.

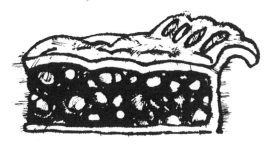

ONION PIE

1 pie crust, unbaked
3 tbsps. butter
2 eggs
½ cup Half & Half
3 medium onions, sliced
1 cup Cheddar cheese
2 tbsps. sour cream
4 strips bacon, fried & drained

Make sure to prick pie crust with a fork. Saute' onions in butter. Place in pie crust. Mix other ingredients together, excluding hot bacon, and place over onions. Cooke at 350⁰ for 30 to 35 minutes. Top with bacon and serve with cold fruit.

FRIED OKRA WITH ONIONS

1 pkg. okra, frozen
1 cup flour
2 tbsps. meal
1 to 4 tbsps. butter
3 medium Vidalia Onions, chopped
1 tsp. salt
4 tbsps. shortening

Melt shortening and heat over medium heat. Mix flour, salt, and meal together and batter okra and onions. When grease is hot, add battered okra and onions. Add batter as needed. Cook until brown. Serve HOT!!

———— • ————

ONION CASSEROLE

5 medium onions, sliced
1 can water chestnuts, sliced &
  drained
2 beaten eggs
1 lb. mushrooms, sliced
1 can cream of chicken soup
1 cup Cheddar cheese
1 can French Fried Onion Rings

Layer first three ingredients. Mix together next 3 ingredients and pour over layers. Bake at 350⁰ F. for 35 to 40 minutes. Top with French Fried Onion Rings and return to oven to brown.

ENGLISH PEA/
ONION CASSEROLE

1 can june peas
1 can cream of chicken soup
1 egg
1½ cups grated cheese, mild American
1 medium Vidalia Onion, chopped
1 can sliced water chestnuts, drained
1½ cups cracker crumbs, Ritz

Mix all ingredients and bake in 350° F. oven for 20 minutes. Serve hot.

———— • ————

ONION RING CASSEROLE

Great for outdoor gas grill!
1 lb. Vidalia Onions
Salt and pepper
⅓ cup water
2 tbsps. butter or margarine
¼ cup milk
1 egg, well beaten
½ cup shredded sharp Cheddar cheese
Paprika

Peel and slice onions ¾-inch thick, separate into rings. Place onion rings in 9-inch foil pan, season to taste with salt and pepper. Add water. Cover snugly with foil. Preheat grill. With cover down, cook on low setting 20 minutes, or until onions are tender. Uncover, dot with butter, stirring as butter melts. Combine milk and eggs, pour over onions. Top with cheese, then sprinkle with paprika. Replace foil. With cover down, cook on low setting 10 minutes or until set.

To cook in oven, cook in a covered casserole dish at 350° F. for 1 hour. Serves 4.
                                Pamela Findlay

ONION BLINTZ CASSEROLE

Filling:
2 lbs. ricotta cheese
3 eggs
¼ cup sugar
Dash of salt
1 lemon or ¼ cup lemon juice
11 oz. cream cheese
2 cups chopped onions
⅛ tsp. lemon rind

Batter:
½ lb. margarine, melted
½ cup sugar
3 eggs
1¼ cups flour
3 tsps. baking powder
⅛ tsp. salt
½ cup milk
1 tsp. vanilla

Mix all ingredients for filling in a mixer, blend well. Set aside. Mix batter ingredients by hand. Spoon ½ batter in a casserole dish. Top with filling, spreading. Do not mix. Spread remaining batter over filling. Bake at 300° F. for 1½ hours. Serve with Canadian Bacon, sausage, or fresh fruit.

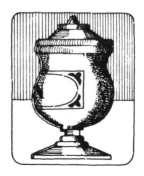

ONIONS AU GRATIN

3½ cups onions, chopped
1½ cups milk
1 tbsp. flour
1 cup grated cheese
4 tbsps. butter
½ tsp. salt
¼ tsp. pepper
Bread crumbs

Saute' onions in 2 tbsps. butter. Arrange a layer of them in an oiled baking dish; cover with milk which has been thickened with the flour and seasoned with butter, salt and pepper, and sprinkle with grated cheese. Repeat until all the ingredients are used, covering the top with buttered bread crumbs. Set in a moderate oven to brown the top nicely and to heat the onions.

ONIONS AND POTATO CASSEROLE

6 large Vidalia Onions, sliced
6 large white potatoes
2 cans condensed mushroom soup
2 lbs. lean ground beef
4 tbsps. fat
2 tbsps. salt on meat

Season meat and brown in hot fat. Peel and slice potatoes thinly. Make alternate layers of potatoes, onions and meat. Pour mushroom soup on top and bake at 350° F. for 45 minutes.

ONIONS BAKED ON COALS

Wrap large, peeled Vidalia Onions in aluminum foil like you do your baked potatoes and bury them in the hot ashes, to come out and go with your baked potato and steak.

GOLDEN ONION RINGS

Cut 6 medium Toombs County Sweet Onions into slices ¼-inch thick. Separate into rings. Combine 1 cup plus 2 tbsps. sifted, all-purpose flour, ½ tsp. salt, 1 slightly beaten egg, 1 cup milk and 2 tbsps. salad oil. Beat together just till dry ingredients are well moistened. Coat onion rings with batter. Fry, a few at a time, in deep hot fat (375° F.) stirring once to separate rings. When onions are golden, drain on paper towels. Just before serving, sprinkle with salt.

———— • ————

ONION CHEESE SOUP

Cook 1 cup chopped onion (1 large) in 3 tbsps. butter till tender but not brown. Blend 3 tbsps. all-purpose flour, ½ tsp. salt, and dash pepper. Add 4 cups milk all at once. Heat and stir till boiling. Remove from heat. Add 2 cups shredded sharp process American cheese, stirring to melt cheese. Serves 4 to 6. Can add fried bread cubes if desired.

———— • ————

ONION CHEESE LOAF

Cut French bread loaf in 1-inch slices cutting **to but not through** bottom of loaf. Combine ⅓ cup butter, softened, and 3 tbsps. prepared mustard; spread over cut surfaces of bread. Insert slices of sharp process American cheese and **thin** slices of onions in slashes. Wrap loaf in foil; heat over **medium** coals about 15 minutes or till hot.

SWISS ONION BAKE

In skillet, melt 2 tbsps. butter; add 2 cups sliced onion and cook till tender. Spread in bottom of 10 x 6 x 1½-inch baking dish. Top onion with 6 hard-cooked eggs, sliced; sprinkle with 6 oz. process Swiss cheese, shredded (1½ cups). Mix one 10½ oz. can condensed cream of chicken soup, ¾ cup milk, and ½ tsp. prepared mustard; heat, stirring till smooth. Pour sauce over casserole being sure some goes to bottom. Place 6 slices French bread, cut ½ inch thick and buttered on top overlapping a little. Bake at 350⁰ F. for 35 minutes or till hot. Broil a few minutes to toast bread. Serves 6.

STUFFED ONION CASSEROLE

6 large Vidalia Onions
1½ cups grated cheese
salt and pepper

Peel onions. Cut a slice from top of each and parboil for 10 minutes. Scoop out the centers, leaving ½-inch thick shell. Chop the centers, adding the cheese, seasoned with salt and pepper. Pack the stuffing into the onion shells. Dot top with butter. Place in baking dish with water to just cover the bottom. Bake, covered, in 350⁰F oven for one hour or until tender. Uncover dish and bake 5 minutes more to slightly brown tops. Garnish with parsley and serve.

STUFFED VIDALIA ONIONS

6 large Vidalia Onions
1½ cups crumbled cornbread
½ cup diced cooked potatoes
1 cup broth (or water)
1 hard boiled egg
1 envelope instant cream of
** chicken soup mix**
Salt & pepper to taste

Peel and wash onions. Simmer in enough water to cover onions for about 10 minutes or until almost tender. Remove pulp from onions, leaving only the two outside layers of the onion. Add onion pulp to other ingredients. Place ingredients in blender and blend for a few seconds for a smooth stuffing. Place onion shells in lightly greased muffin tins or custard cups. Fill with stuffing and sprinkle with paprika. Bake in slow oven 325⁰ F. for about 30 minutes. To serve, place stuffed onions around meat.

Effie Purvis

SAUTEÉD ONIONS

4 onions, sliced ¼-inch thick
3 tbsps. butter or margarine

Preheat Multi-Cooker Frypan to 300⁰ F. Add butter and melt. Add onions and saute', stirring frequently until golden in color. Sprinkle with salt. Serve over chops, hamburgers, steak or liver, etc. 4 servings.

STUFFED VIDALIA ONION CASSEROLE

3 cups chopped boiled chicken
½ cup raw rice, to be cooked in chicken broth
½ cup chopped celery
½ lb. mushrooms - sliced
6 medium Vidalia Onions
1 can cream of mushroom soup
1 tsp. cooking oil
Salt & pepper to taste

Core center of onions after peeling. Reserve enough of onion centers (approximately 1 cup) to saute' with mushrooms and celery in cooking oil. Add chopped chicken, cooked rice, and salt and pepper to taste. Stuff cored onions with mixture. Place in slightly greased 2-qt. baking dish. Place remaining stuffing mixture over and around onions. Combine soup with enough water to rinse can. Pour soup and water over casserole. Bake in preheated 350ºF oven until soup is bubbling. Onions should remain crunchy.   Charlotte Grimes

GLAZED VIDALIA ONIONS

4 large Vidalia Onions
¼ cup vinegar
¼ cup honey
2 tbsps. oil
1 tsp. dry mustard
½ tsp. salt
½ tsp. paprika

Peel onions. Cut in half and place cut side up in a single layer in skillet. Add water to almost cover -- salt well. Combine rest of ingredients. Pour over onions and simmer for 30 minutes. Baste to glaze. Remove onions, bring sauce to a boil and spoon over onions. Serves 8.
Mrs. Carolyn Darby

CHARCOAL BAKED ONIONS SUPREME

6 medium-size sweet onions
1½ cups prepared stuffing mix
1 tsp. poultry seasoning (optional)
1½ cups grated sharp cheese
¾ cup melted butter or margarine
1/3 cup hot water

Peel onions and cut each crosswise in 3 or 4 thick slices. Combine stuffing mix and cheese, add melted butter and hot water along with poultry seasoning if desired. Blend well. Spread stuffing mixture thickly between onion slices, reassemble each onion. Wrap each onion securely in heavy aluminum foil or double thickness of regular foil. Place on grill or directly on coals. Bake 1 or 2 hours, depending on size of onions and heat of fire.

PIMENTO-ONION RELISH

1/3 cup vinegar
½ tsp. fine herbs
2 tbsps. sugar
2/3 cup water
1-4-oz. can or jar whole pimentos quartered
1 medium onion, thinly sliced (about 1 cup)

Combine vinegar, fine herbs, sugar and water. Add pimentos and onion; marinate overnight. Drain; serve with meat.

60

ONION AND ZUCCHINI CASSEROLE

1-14 oz. can Hunt's Stewed Tomatoes
1 large can kernel corn (drained)
1-16 oz. can tomato paste
3 stalkes celery (diced)
1½ lbs. ground beef
3-6 fresh zucchini medium round slices
3 Vidalia Onions (medium)
½-lb. sharp cheddar cheese (grated)
1 pkg. egg noodles
3 garlic cloves (pressed)
Salt & Pepper to taste

Boil egg noodles according to package. Cook ground beef, garlic and celery together until ground beef is done and celery semi-soft. When completed - drain. Then add corn, tomato paste, and stewed tomatoes to mixture. (Be sure to leave juice on tomatoes). Grate cheese, slice zucchini and onions into round slices. Layer in a large greased casserole dish; 1) noodles, 2) meat mixture, 3) onion slices, 4) zucchini slices, 5) cheese. Repeat layering once. Cover and bake in moderate oven until onions are tender. The last few minutes you may want to uncover and brown cheese on top.

ONION CASSEROLE

1 lb. sharp cheese
3 lbs. Vidalia Onions
1-14 oz. bottle Heinz Ketchup
Salt & Pepper to taste

Peel and slice onions about ½" thick. Boil until tender and drain. Grate cheese. Layer in casserole dish starting with onions, then cheese, salt and pepper and cover with ketchup. Make into two layers. Place in hot oven (about 400°F) for 20 minutes or until cheese has thoroughly melted.   Anita Estroff

MEXI - YUMS

6 Vidalia jumbo onions
1 can chili with beans (or equivalant amount of your own chili)
½ lb. sharp cheddar cheese
1 avocado (very ripe)
1 bag fritos or nacho cheese doritos

Peel onions, place in boiling salt water enough to cover onions and boil 15 minutes. Remove and rinse in cold water. Remove centers of onion leaving two or three of the outside layers. Chop centers and mix with chili and most of grated cheese. Mash avocado. Place onions in a greased casserole dish. Refill shells with chili mixture until almost full. On top of that place 1 - 1 tbsps. of mashed avocado. Sprinkle remainder of grated cheese on top of all onions. Bake at 350°F for 20 to 30 minutes or until onions are tender. Serve each onion over a bed of fritos or doritos. Serving suggestions: Try cold Gazpacho with sour cream to make a complete lunch or dinner. Serves 6.   Sheri Threlkeld

ONION PIE

10 to 12 saltine crackers
1 lb. onions, sliced thin
1/3 stick margarine

Melt margarine and pour half into crushed crackers. Blend well and press into pie tin. Saute' onions in remaining margarine until tender but not brown. Put onions on pie crust and pour over call a cup of white sauce to which ¼ lb. of melted sharp cheese has been added. Sprinkle a few cracker crumbs over top. Bake at 350°F for about 15 minutes.

ONION-BROCCOLI DELUXE

2-10 oz. pkgs. frozen broccoli, spears
2 cups Vidalia Onions, small
3 tbsps. butter or margarine
3 tbsps. all purpose flour, sifted
¼ tsp. salt
⅛ tsp. pepper, black
¾ cup milk
1-8 oz. pkg. cream cheese, cut up
1 small bag toasted sliced almonds

In saucepan cook broccoli and onions in boiling salted water about 7 minutes or until tender; drain.

In a saucepan melt margarine; blend in flour, salt, pepper. Add milk and cook until thick and bubbly. Beat cream cheese 4 minutes or until smooth and slowly add flour mixture.

Line broccoli onion mixture in casserole dish and top with cream cheese mixture and place in 1½-qt. casserole. Bake, uncovered, in a 350°F oven 30 to 35 minutes. Sprinkle with almonds. Makes 8 servings.

———— • ————

QUICK POTATOES & ONIONS

1 large can small, whole potatoes
1½ cups chopped Vidalia Onions
¼ lb. butter or margarine
Parsley

Drain and rinse canned potatoes. Arrange in greased loaf pan. Melt butter and add chopped onions. Pour butter and onions over potatoes. Garnish with parsley and bake in 400°F oven 20 to 30 minutes, or until lightly browned. Paprika may be sprinkled on top for added color. If desired.

VIDALIA ONION SUPREME

1 baked pie shell
3 cups thinly sliced Vidalia Onions
3 tbsps. melted butter
½ cup milk
1½ cups sour cream
1 tsp. salt
2 eggs (well beaten)
3 tbsps. flour
Bacon slices

Cook onion in butter until lightly browned; spoon into pastry shell. Add milk, 1¼ cups sour cream. Blend flour with ¼ cup sour cream. Combine with egg mixture; pour over onion mixture. Bake in slow oven (325°F) for 30 minutes or until firm in center. Garnish with crisp fried bacon. Optional: Parsley flakes may be sprinkled on top before baking. Serves 6 to 8.   Mrs. Franklin Conner

VIDALIA ONION CHEESE PIE

1 qt. Vidalia Onions, thinly sliced
½ qt. eggs (lightly beaten)
1/3 quart milk
½ tsp. salt
5 1/3 oz. cheese, grated
½ tsp. nutmeg, thyme
2 1/3 oz. bread crumbs

Steam onions for five minutes. Scald milk, remove from heat. Add cheese and stir until melted. Add seasonings and lightly beaten eggs. Line 9-inch pie pan with pastry and bake until slightly browned. Sprinkle a few bread crumbs in the bottom of each crust. Distribute onions evenly over bottom of crust. Pour milk mixture over onions. Sprinkle with cheese and crumbs on top. Bake at 325°F or 163°C until the custard is set and the pies lightly browned.

BAKED VIDALIA ONIONS IN SHERRY CREAM SAUCE

3 cups pre-cooked Vidalia Onions
1 cup light cream
2 tbsps. pimento
½ tsp. salt
⅛ tsp. pepper
1 small jar sliced mushrooms
⅓ cup sherry
3 tbsps. butter
⅓ cup sharp Cheddar cheese

Drain onions, arrange in shallow baking dish. Combine sherry, light cream, salt, pepper, pimentos and mushrooms. Pour over onions, dot with butter. Sprinkle with grated cheese, cover and bake at 350⁰ F. for 20 minutes. Option: This recipe can also be made using sour cream.

Mrs. Bessie Harrelson

————— • —————

VIDALIA ONIONS WITH CHEESE SAUCE

12 medium Vidalia Onions
1 tsp. salt
4 tbsps. butter
4 tbsps. flour
2 cups milk
Paprika
2 hard boiled eggs, grated
1 cup grated cheese
½ tsp. Worcestershire Sauce
Parsley

Peel onions; cook in boiling, salted water until tender. Drain and cool. Place onions in dish. Set aside. In top of double boiler, blend butter and flour thoroughly; add liquid gradually, stirring constantly. Add grated cheese and Worcestershire

Sauce. Cover tightly and place over hot water until ready to use. Pour over Vidalia Onions. Garnish with grated eggs, parsley and paprika. Serves 6.

Mrs. C. L. Hall, Jr.

————— • —————

VEGETABLES WITH ONION SAUCE

1 pkg. frozen French cut green beans
1 pkg. frozen baby lima beans
1 pkg. frozen green peas

Cook each vegetable separately, drain and season. Layer hot vegetables in casserole. Top with sauce.
SAUCE:
1½ cup mayonnaise
3 hard boiled eggs, quartered
1 tsp. Worcestershire Sauce
1 onion, quartered
1 tsp. prepared mustard
Juice of 1 lemon
dash of garlic salt
dash of Tabasco Sauce

Mix all ingredients in blender. Make sauce at least one day ahead and store in refrigerator. Complete dish may be warmed in oven at 300⁰ F. if necessary. May be served cold. Yield: 8-10 servings.

Mrs. Robert P. Thompson

ONION PIE
Delicious!

1 cup finely crumbled Ritz crackers
½ stick butter, melted
2 cups Vidalia Onions, thinly sliced
2 tsps. butter
2 eggs
¾ cup milk
¾ tsp. salt
Dash pepper
¼ cup grated sharp Cheddar cheese
Paprika
Parsley

Mix cracker crumbs with melted butter, press into 8-inch pie plate. Saute' onions in 2 tbsps. butter until clear, but not brown. Spoon into crust. Beat eggs together with milk, salt, pepper and pour over onions. Sprinkle with cheese and paprika. Bake at 350⁰ F. for 30 minutes or until a knife inserted in the center comes out clean. Sprinkle with parsley before serving. Serves 6-8.

Pamela Findlay

FRENCH FRIED
ONION RINGS

1 cup flour
1 cup beer
2 large Vidalia Onions
2 tbsps. meal
¾ tsp. salt
4 cups oil

Combine flour, meal, beer and salt in a bowl using a swish. Cool and let sit 3 to 3½ hours at room temperature. 30 minutes before batter is ready, preheat oven to 200⁰ F. Heat oil and batter onion rings. Fry in grease until brown and place in casserole dish (DON'T STACK) until golden brown and crispy. Can freeze.

ZUCCHINI CASSEROLE

2 squash
1 pint tomatoes
3 tbsps. sugar
1 green pepper (optional)
3 tbsps. flour
1 tsp. salt
1 medium onion
½ tsp. oregano

Top with: 3 tbsps. butter
1 cup bread crumbs
4 oz. sharp cheese

Dice or slice squash. Cook in boiling water 5 minutes. Dice onions and pepper. Brown onion and pepper in butter. Stir in flour and tomatoes. Stir over low heat until thickened. Add salt and sugar. Layer drained squash into buttered 2 qt. casserole. Pour on tomato mixture. Top wtih grated cheese, bread crumbs, and dot with butter. Bake 350⁰ F. for about 45 minutes or until golden brown.

Mrs. Robert P. Thompson

GRILLED ONIONS

Peel the onion, sprinkle on salt and pepper, add a good hunk of butter then wrap it in tin foil and bake at 350⁰ F. until tender.

Microwave Recipes

CRAB MEAT CANAPÉS

6 oz. shredded crab meat
1 cup mayonnaise
½ tsp. lemon juice
¼ cup chopped Vidalia Onions
1 egg white
Ritz crackers

In a small mixing bowl, combine crab meat with mayonnaise and season with lemon juice. Beat egg white until stiff (not dry) and fold in crab meat mixture. Place approximately 1 tsp. crab mixture on each Ritz cracker and cook 45 to 60 seconds, or until heated thoroughly. Serve immediately. Yield: 25 canapés.

CHEESE PUFFS

1 8-oz. pkg. cream cheese, room temp.
1 egg yolk
2 tsps. minced Vidalia Onions
1 tsp. baking powder
3 tbsps. imitation bacon bits
30 Melba Toasts Rounds

In a large bowl, beat cream cheese until creamy. Add egg yolk, onion and baking powder, mixing well after each addition. Add bacon bits. Place 1 tsp. cheese mixture on each cracker and cook for 25 to 30 seconds, or until slightly risen. Serve immediately. Yield: 30 appetizers.

ONION BREAD

1 8½-oz. pkg. corn muffin mix
⅔ cup biscuit baking mix
⅔ cup milk, evaporated
1 egg
1 medium onion, chopped

In a large mixing bowl, combine corn muffin mix, biscuit baking mix, milk, egg and onion. Spray a 9 x 2-inch dish with PAM. Pour batter in dish and bake in microwave 3 to 4 minutes, until toothpick come out clean. Let stand 10 minutes in microwave.

ONION SAUCE

2 tbsps. butter or margarine
2 onions, medium, chopped
¼ cup butter or margarine, melted
¼ cup all-purpose flour, sifted
½ tsp. salt
½ tsp. seasoned salt
¼ tsp. paprika
2 cups milk
1 tsp. Worcestershire Sauce

Melt margarine and saute' onions. Set aside. In a saucepan, combine butter and margarine, flour, salt, seasoned salt and paprika. Mix milk and Worcestershire Sauce. Add to saucepan all at once. Cook and stir mixture till thick and bubbly. Add saute'ed onions and mix together. Makes about 2 cups.

VIDALIA ONION SOUP

2 medium Vidalia Onions, thinly sliced
2 tbsps. margarine or butter
2 14-oz. each can of beef broth
¼ cup water
1 tsp. Worcestershire Sauce
4 slices Mozzarella cheese,
   halved or shredded
3 slices bread
1 tsp. garlic salt
½ tsp. seasoning salt
3 tsps. grated Parmesan cheese

Place onions and butter in a 3 qt. casserole dish. Cook in microwave 8 to 10 minutes, or until onion is tender. Add broth, water and Worcestershire Sauce. Cook covered for 5 to 7 minutes or until mixture boils. Cut up bread into ¼ x ¼ inch pieces and add garlic salt and seasoning salt and toast in oven. Place on paper towel and sprinkle with Parmesan cheese. Heat in microwave 15 to 30 seconds or until cheese is softened. Pour soup in bowl and place bread cubes on top. Serve immediately. Yield: 4 servings.

————— • —————

BAR-B-QUE SAUCE

½ cup catsup
1 tsp. dry mustard
2 dashes Tabasco
1 tbsp. Worcestershire Sauce
½ cup minced Vidalia Onions
⅛ cup margarine or oil

Mix together and serve on franks, hamburgers, cube steaks, chicken, etc. Makes about ¾ cup.

LIVER AND ONIONS

¾ lb. calf liver, sliced ¼ inch thick
¼ cup flour
½ tsp. salt
¼ tsp. red pepper
¼ tsp. paprika
¼ to ½ cup oil
½ to 1 cup water
3 Vidalia Onions, sliced
4 tbsps. flour

Heat oil in skillet. Sift flour, salt, pepper and paprika together. Batter liver in flour mixture and fry about 4 minutes. Overcooking makes liver tough and hard. Remove liver and save 2 tbsps. grease, while hot add flour, (to desired brown color) and add water to make a gravy. Pour gravy over liver in a casserole dish, placing onion on top. Cook in 350° F. oven 25 to 30 minutes. Approximately 4 servings.

————— • —————

CHILI SAUCE

4 tsps. whole cloves
2 tbsps. whole allspice
4 qts. chopped, peeled ripe tomatoes
   (8 lbs.)
2½ cups chopped medium Vidalia Onions
2 cups chopped seeded green and red
   sweet peppers (5)
1½ cups granulated sugar
1½ tbsps. salt
1 qt. cider vinegar

Tie spices in cheese cloth; add the rest of the ingredients in saucepan. Cook, uncovered, stirring often, 2½ to 3 hours, or until very thick. Remove spice bag. Can process in jars if so desired. Makes 4 to 5 pints.

CHICKEN TETRAZZINE

4 oz. spaghetti, broken into 2-inch
  lengths and cooked
1 10¾ oz. cream of chicken soup
½ cup evaporated milk
1 tbsp. margarine or butter
1 cup shredded cheddar cheese
1 6½ to 7 oz. can chicken, drained
1 3 oz. can sliced mushrooms, drained
1 small Vidalia Onion, chopped

Combine cooked spaghetti, soup and milk in a 2-qt. casserole dish. Blend in chicken, mushrooms, onion and ½ cup cheese. Mix lightly and cover. Cook in Microwave 8 minutes. Stir halfway through cooking time. Sprinkle on remaining cheese and cook 1 to 2 minutes, or until cheese is melted. 6 servings.

———— • ————

ONION CASSEROLE

4 medium onions, sliced
3 tbsps. butter or margarine
1 2½ oz. can sliced mushrooms, drained
1 tsp. paprika
1½ cups plain croutons
½ cup shredded caraway seed cheese
½ cup shredded mild cheddar cheese
3 tbsps. grated Parmesan cheese
1 10¾ oz. cream of chicken soup

Place onion and butter in a 3 qt. casserole dish. Cook 7 to 10 minutes, until tender. Stir halfway through cooking time. Blend cream of chicken soup, paprika, and mushrooms and cook 2 minutes. Toss croutons with butter. Spoon over onion mixture. Sprinkle with cheeses, season with paprika as desired. Cook 1 to 2 minutes or until cheese is melted.

"SOUPER" RICE

1¼ cups water
¾ tsp. instant beef bouillon
1¼ cups quick cooking rice
1 10 oz. cream of chicken soup
1 small Vidalia Onion, chopped
1 small can mushrooms, drained

Combine water and beef bouillon in a 2 qt. casserole dish. Cook 2½ minutes or until mixture boils. Stir in rice. Let stand, covered until water is absorbed. Stir in soup, onions, and mushrooms and cook 3 minutes or until heated thoroughly. Serve immediately. 6 servings.

———— • ————

LASAGNA

1 lb. ground beef
1 medium Vidalia Onion, chopped
¼ tsp. garlic salt
½ tsp. salt
¼ tsp. pepper
1 large can mushrooms, drained & sliced
1 tsp. oregano
½ tsp. basil
½ lb. shredded Mozzarella cheese
1 lb. shredded cheddar cheese
1 medium bell pepper
2 8-oz. cans of tomato sauce
½ lb. cooked lasagna noodles
Parmesan cheese

Combine ground beef, bell pepper, onion, and garlic salt in a 3 qt. casserole dish. Cook 3 to 4 minutes and stir 1 or 2 times during cooking time. Blend in salt, pepper, oregano, basil and tomato sauce. Cook 10 minutes. Stir halfway through cooking time. Add mushrooms. Layer meat mixture, noodles, and mixed cheese. Repeat layers ending with meat sauce. Sprinkle top generously with Parmesan cheese, as desired. Cook covered 12 to 14 minutes. 12 servings.

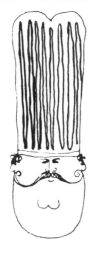

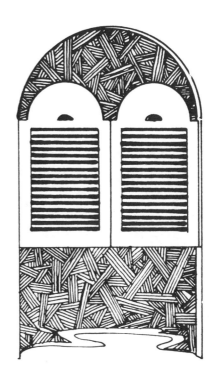

OMELET

9 to 10 slices (½ lb.) bacon
1 medium Vidalia Onion, chopped
8 eggs, beaten
¼ cup evaporated milk
¼ tsp. pepper
salt
½ cup grated cheddar cheese

Cook bacon 8 to 9 minutes until crisp. Remove and crumble. Remove all grease, reserving 1 tbsp. Add onions to grease and cook 1 minute or until tender. Mix together eggs, bacon, onion, cheddar cheese, and seasonings. Season with salt, as desired. Pour into pie plate and cook 6 to 7 minutes or until firm, not moist. Serve immediately. 4 servings.

Nutritional Information, Weights & Measurements, Conversions

NUTRITION

You are what you eat.

Your nutrition can determine how you look, feel and act; whether you are homely or beautiful, grouchy or cheerful, enjoy your work or make it a drudgery, increase your earning power or stay in an economic rut.

Good nutrition promotes good health. Nutrition has been defined as: "the food you eat and how your body uses it".

Nutrient needs of healthy individuals vary with body size, physical activity, growth, substances lost from the body, metabolic rate and age. Use a wide variety of foods for essential nutrients. Infants and children require more nutrients per kilogram of body weight than do adults. Women in the child-bearing years have high iron requirements. Pregnancy is a time of growth and increased body size. Senior citizens have about the same nutritional needs as do younger adults of comparable size, but their need for calories is comparably less.

———— • ————

IMPORTANT VITAMINS:

1. Vitamin A -
   Natural Sources: Yellow fruits, dark green, leafy vegetables, liver, fish liver oil, butter, egg yolk, and milk.
   Functions: Builds resistance to infection, promotes growth and vitality. Promotes healthy skin. Essential for pregnancy.

2. Vitamin B - Thiamin
   Natural Sources: Dried yeast, whole wheat, oatmeal, peanuts, lean pork, milk, most vegetables, egg yolk, liver and other organ meats.
   Functions: Promotes growth and digestion. Necessary for normal functioning of nerves.

3. Vitamin C - Ascorbic Acid
   Natural Sources: Citrus fruits, strawberries, greens, cabbage family, green pepper (easily destroyed by cooking).
   Functions: Necessary for healthy teeth, gums and bones; promotes wound healing and very important in maintaining sound health and vigor.

4. Vitamin B^2 - Riboflavin
   Natural Sources: Cheese, eggs, yeast, liver, kidney, lean meats, milk and most B^1 sources.
   Functions: Improves growth and development essential for normal vision, mouth and skin tone; promotes general health.

5. Vitamin B^6 - Pyridoxine
   Natural Sources: Muscle meats, liver, kidneys and organ meats, fish, milk, egg yolk, yeast, cantaloupe, cabbage, peanuts, whole-grain cereals, soybeans and green vegetables.
   Functions: Prevents nausea and vomiting during pregnancy and aids in food assimilation. Prevents various nervous skin disorders.

6. Vitamin B^{12} - Cobalomin "Red Vitamin"
   Natural Sources: Meat, liver, beef, pork, fish, milk, eggs and cheese.
   Functions: Prevents • Anemia promotes growth and increased appetite in children. Normal functions of nervous tissue and gastrointestinal tact.
   • Anemia - Anemia is due to a

deficiency (lack) of nutrients necessary in the formation of blood.

7. Vitamin D - "Sunshine Vitamin"

    Natural Sources: Fish liver oils, fat, Vitamin D fortified milk, egg yolks, butter, sardines, salmon, and sunshine.

    Functions: Proper formation of bones and teeth. Very important in infancy and childhood.

8. Vitamin E -

    Natural Sources: Egg yolks, liver, meat, vegetable oils (wheat germ, corn soybean, cotton seed), whole wheat, green leafy vegetables, nuts, legumes, and margarine.

    Functions: Exact function in humans is not yet known. Medical articles have been published on its value in helping to prevent sterility.

9. Vitamin K -

    Natural Sources: Alfalfa and other green, leafy vegetables, soybean oil, egg yolks.

    Functions: Important in blood clotting and liver function.

10. Nicotinic Acid - Niacin

    Natural Sources: Organ meats, pork liver, lean meat, poultry, fish, enriched rice, whole wheat products, yeast, green vegetables, beans, peanuts.

    Functions: Used to lower blood cholesterol levels. Promotes growth and normal skin conditions.

11. Pantothenic Acid - "From Everywhere"

    Natural Sources: Liver, kidney, yeast, wheat, bran, peas, crude molasses.

    Functions: Necessary for the maintenance of normal skin and development of the central nervous system. Originally believed to be a factor in restoring gray hair to original color. This function has not been substantiated.

12. Folic Acid -

    Natural Sources: Deep green leafy vegetables, dried beans, nuts, cereals, liver, kidney, yeast, lean beef.

    Functions: Contributes to normal growth; necessary for regeneration of red blood cells.

13. Choline -

    Natural Sources: Liver, yeast, wheat germ, egg yolks, brain, heart, green leafy vegetables, legumes.

    Functions: Regulates liver function.

14. Inositol -

    Natural Sources: Milk, meat, yeast, fruit, nuts, whole grains.

    Functions: Similar to that of choline.

15. Biotin -

    Natural Sources: Liver, eggs, fish, muscle meat, milk, whole-grain cereals, legumes, nuts, most fats and vegetables.

    Functions: Growth-promoting factor.

IMPORTANT MINERALS:

1. **Calcium** - Builds and maintains bones and teeth; helps clot blood, regular heart rhythm, vitality and endurance.

2. **Cobalt** - Component of Vitamin B^{12}, normal growth of appetite.

3. **Copper** - Prevents anemia.

4. **Flourine** - May decrease dental cavities.
5. **Iodine** - Necessary for normal function of thyroid gland, proper growth.
6. **Iron** - Blood formation and prevents anemia.
7. **Magnesium** - Necessary for Calcium and Vitamin C, normal function of nervous and muscular system.
8. **Manganese** - Proper utilization of Vitamin B^1 and Vitamin E.
9. **Molybdenum** - Carbohydrate (sugars and starches) metabolism.
10. **Phosphorus** - Normal bone and teeth structure. Interrelated with Calcium and Vitamin D "sunshine Vitamin".
11. **Potassium** - Normal muscle tone, nerves, heart action.
12. **Sulphur** - Good skin, hair, and nails.
13. **Zinc** - Normal protein and carbohydrate metabolism, muscle movement.

FOODS WHICH CONTAIN:

(Pro) Protein	(Fe) Iron
Meat	Celery
Fish	Oranges
Nuts	Fish
Milk	Apples
Eggs	Cheese
Peanut Butter	Canned Tomatoes
Cheese	Canned Asparagus
Corn Meal	Cauliflower
Dried Peas	Carrots
Dried Beans	Canned Peas
Oatmeal	Bananas
Bread	Meat

Wheat Cereal
Macaroni
Rice

Eggs
Prunes
String Beans
Lettuce
Turnips
Dried Peas
Raisins
Oatmeal
Potatoes
Spinach
Dried Beans
Cabbage

(Ca+) CALCIUM	(P) PHOSPHORUS
Cabbage	Dried Beans
Meat	Rhubarb
Milk	Fish
Spinach	Turnips
Oatmeal	Cheese
Turnips	Dried Peas
Potatoes	Cauliflower
Cheese	Carrots
Fish	Oatmeal
Eggs	Prunes
Carrots	Spinach
Cauliflower	Celery
Bananas	Oranges
Oranges	Potatoes
Celery	Eggs
Canned Peas	Bananas
Dried Beans	Milk
String Beans	Meat
Canned Tomatoes	
Rhubarb	
Asparagus	

GOALS OF MEAL PLANNING:

1. Serve attractive and appetizing food.
2. Variety of foods from the basic four food groups to meet each individual

family member's nutritional needs.
3. Keep within the food budget.
4. Plan meals in advance with menus.

WAYS TO REDUCE PROTEIN COSTS:

1. Use small servings of meat, poultry and fish.
2. Use lower grades and less tender cuts of meat.
3. Use legumes, peanut butter and eggs for some meals.

WISE FOOD PURCHASES:

1. Plan menus for a week at a time.
2. Make and go by a shopping list.
3. Use and stay within a budget.
4. Checks ads to find bargains.
5. Compare labels to get good nutritional values.
6. Compare prices and grades.
7. Check dates for fresh foods.
8. Understand grades and cuts of meats and use this in selecting meats.
9. Do not buy overpriced foods.
10. Return spoiled or damaged products.

SELECTION OF ONIONS

Onions, dry	Bright, clean, hard, well-shaped globes with dry skins. (A thick, tough woody condition indicates poor quality.)
Onions, green	Crisp, tender green tops. (Yellowing, wilted, or discolored tops are undesirable.)
Onions, green: leeks	Green fresh tops; crisp, young, tender bulbs. (Yellow top indicates over maturity.)
Onions, green: shallots	Crisp, straight stems; slight bulb development. (Tough or fiberous necks indicate over maturity.)

————— • —————

COOKERY TERMS

A la, au, aux - Simply means as it is served.

Aspic - Savory jelly made with a stock.

Au gratin - With a cheese sauce.

Au naturel - In its natural state.

Bechamel - A sauce made with stock and milk or cream.

Bisque - A term applied both to soup and ice cream. Applied to soup with a cream sauce and to ice cream to which is added finely chopped nuts.

Blanch - To scald, to whiten.

Bombeglace' - Molded ice cream and ice, or two types of ice cream, the outside of one kind and the inside of another.

Braise - To stew in a covered pan.

Cafe' au lait - Coffee with hot milk.

Cafe' noir - Black coffee.

Canape' -Pieces of toast or bread spread with some appetizing mixture. Served as a first course at a formal lunch or dinner.

Cannelon - A roll, either of veal or beef, or else of baked puff paste.

Caviar - Salted roe from a large fish like a sturgeon.

Charlotte - A pudding. It is made of strips of bread or cake covered with a fruit or gelatin.

Compote - Fruit stewed in syrup.

Consomme' - Very rich stock

Cre'ole, a'al - Cooked with tomatoes.

Croustade - A crispy patty to hold a filling. It may be of bread or rice.

Cutlets - Steaks of veal, lamb, mutton, or pork.

Demitasse - A term applied both to a half size cup and the coffee which it holds.

En coquilles - In shells. Example: Halibut en coquilles means that small pieces of fish are baked on shells. Real scallop shells are charming, and china imitations of them are also used.

Entree' - A main dish, served between courses or as a course by itself.

Farci - Stuffed eggs.

Fillet - Long thin pieces of meat or fish.

Foie Gras - Fat liver, liver of specially fattened geese.

Frappe'- Half frozen, or frozen to a mush.

Glace' - Iced or glossed over.

Haricot - A bean. A stew in which meat and vegetables are finely divided.

Jardiniere - Mixed vegetables.

Lardoon - Small pieces of salt pork or bacon used in frying or inserted in the top of a roast to add succulent flavor.

Macedoine - Mixture of several kinds of fruits or vegetables.

Pot au feu - The pot on the fire.

Ragout - A sort of stew. Meat simmered with vegetables and highly seasoned.

Re'chaufee - Warmed again.

Roux - Thickening made by blending flour and melted butter.

Saute' - Is applied to the process of frying quickly in a small amount of fat, turning to brown evenly all over.

Souffle' - "Puffed up". A dish, served hot, made with eggs, milk, and flour, beaten light and combined with potato, cheese, fruit or other flavoring. The dish has a delightful fluffy texture.

Timbale - A mixture of fish or cheese, or vegetables cooked in a special drum case. Also applied to a pastry case fried in deep fat on an iron especially designed for this purpose.

Veloute' - A sauce made of white stock instead of milk. Vegetables and seasonings should be boiled in the stock to give it flavorings, then strained.

Vol-au-vent - A light puff paste with border high enough to hold a ragout.

VOLUME

Household Measurements

1 cup (c)

tablespoons (Tbsps)
tablespoon (Tbsp)
teaspoon (Tsp)
quart (qt)
pint (pt)

WEIGHT

L = Liter
Ml = milliliter
L) 10 deciliters (d) =
milliliters (ml) or 1000 cc
pound (1 lb. or #) = 0.45 kg
oz. = 28 grams = 30 gm.
kg. = 2.2 lbs.
g. = kilogram
To convert lbs. to kg, divide lb. by 2.2
or multiply times 0.45.

To convert kg. to lb., multiply kg. times
.2
gram = 0.035 oz.
kilogram = 2.2 lbs.
oz. = 30 grams
lb. = 454 grams

TEMPERATURE

To convert Celsius (C) to Fahrenheit (F),
C = 5/9 (^{0}F - 32)
Subtract 32, then multiply times
/9)
To convert Fah. to Cel., ^{0}F = 5/9^{0}C + 32
Multiply times 5/9, then add 32)
Centigrade = 5/9 (^{0}F - 32)
Fahrenheit = 9/5 (^{0}C + 32)

EQUIVALENT COMMON
FOOD MEASURES

T. = 3 t.
½ fluid ounces
14.8 milliliters
fluid ounces = 2 T
8 cup

1 lb. = 16 oz.
  2 liquid cups
¼ cup = 4 T
⅓ cup = 5⅓ T
½ cup = 8 T
⅔ cup = 10⅔ T
¾ cup = 12 T
1 c = 16 T
  8 fluid oz.
  236.6 milliliters
1 gill = ½ cup
1 pt = 2 cups
1 qt = 2 pts
1 gallon = 4 qts
1 peck = 8 qts
1 bushel = 4 pecks

OVEN TEMPERATURES

Very slow oven - 250 - 275^0 F
Slow oven - 300 - 325^0 F
Moderate oven - 350 - 375^0 F
Hot oven - 400 - 425^0 F
Very Hot oven - 450 - 475^0 F
Extremely Hot oven - 500 - 525^0 F

ABBREVIATIONS

tsp - teaspoon
tbsp - tablespoon
c - cup
pt - pint
qt - quart
gal - gallon
oz - ounce

fl oz - fluid ounce

lb - pound

bu - bushel

pk - peck

pkg - package

mg - milligram

gm - gram

kg - kilogram

ml - milliliter

l - liter

^{0}F - degrees Fahrenheit

^{0}C - degrees Centigrade

INDEX

W

Z

Design, Typesetting and Layout done by
GRAPHIC ARTS, PWS
Vidalia, GA 30474.